A Question of the Black Country

A Question of the Black Country

The quiz book that is also a history book

ANDREW HOMER

Tin Typewriter

Tin Typewriter Publishing

Copyright © 2021 Andrew Homer

First published 2021
Tin Typewriter Publishing
Sedgley
www.tintypewriter.com

ISBN: 9798465803298

CONTENTS

Introduction

The Black Country is something of an enigma. Nobody can agree on where its actual borders are or indeed why it is called the Black Country. Even the Ordnance Survey in 2009 when they decided to name the area, stated officially that they were not going to draw a border around it because nobody in the Black Country would agree where it should be! Instead, they opted for simply placing the words Black Country between Dudley and West Bromwich.

It is the border towns that generate the most controversy. Wolverhampton in particular seems to divide people between those who are adamant it is not part of the Black Country and those who are equally adamant that it is. The Black Country has its own unique dialect, a way of speaking that can be traced back to Anglo-Saxon times. This dialect is generally spoken within an area roughly constrained by Wolverhampton to the north, Walsall, West Bromwich, and Smethwick to the east, moving round to Halesowen and Stourbridge to the south, with Kingswinford and Himley to the west. In the author's opinion where the dialect was or is still commonly spoken, there we have the real Black Country.

The one thing that Black Country folk will agree on is that Birmingham is not, never has been, and never will be part of the Black Country! Even so, links go back a long way. Birmingham had scant mineral resources of its own which is why the first canal between the two areas was created to transport mainly coal into industrial Birmingham. Birmingham's famous gun trade relied heavily on Black Country craftsmen to supply precision parts. The Black Country is now recognised as a UNESCO Global Geopark in recognition of our wonderful geological and cultural heritage.

This quiz book contains 200 questions in 20 different categories covering a wide range of topics celebrating the people, places, industry, and heritage that makes the region known as the Black Country so unique. The answer sections contain both the answers, as would be expected in a quiz book, and also more detailed explanations making this as much a history book as a quiz book. Many of the questions will fall within living memory for many people but will still make you think!

The Black Country

The Black Country

Despite having no clearly defined borders, people in the Black Country know exactly where it is and where the name comes from. Of course, getting everyone to agree is another matter altogether. Hopefully, this first section will not be the cause of too many arguments!

1. What is the generally accepted reason for this area being called the Black Country?

2. Which 1846 publication first included Black Country in the title?

3. Who was Elihu Burritt?

4. What was the name of Elihu Burritt's 1868 book on the Black Country?

5. The Black Country has its own recognized regional flag but who designed it?

6. What industries are represented on the Black Country flag?

7. Which four boroughs make up the present-day Black Country?

8. What minerals, found extensively in the Black Country, were needed for making iron?

9. Wrens Nest Nature Reserve in Dudley is internationally famous for what?

10. Which two rivers in the Black Country flow into the River Severn and the River Trent respectively?

Question 6 – The Black Country Flag

Answers – Section 1

1. The vast amount of smoke, dust and pollution making everything black

There is some debate over the origins of the name Black Country although the generally accepted reason is the amount of pollution, smoke, and dust being belched out by the industry making everything black. Another view involves the South Staffordshire Coalfield, which the Black Country sits on. Early mining maps tended to shade this grey or black. Even so, the name most likely derives from the abundance of mineral resources and the uses they were put to in a relatively small, heavily industrialised area.

2. 'Colton Green, a tale of the Black Country', by Reverend William Gresley

Colton Green was published in 1846 but it was not the first time the Black Country had appeared in print. The Staffordshire Advertiser on the 27th of November 1841 contained a report entitled 'Reform Dinner at Lichfield'. The Town Clerk, Mr Simpson, referred to 'the black country in Staffordshire – Wolverhampton, Bilston and Tipton – which latter place, a minister of former times had described as a little village with gurgling brook'. Apparently, the audience laughed at this description of Tipton! No doubt the name 'Black Country' had been in use, at least colloquially, long before 1841.

3. The United States Consul in Birmingham

Elihu Burritt was born in Connecticut and was nicknamed the 'Learned Blacksmith' for his natural scholarship. He was a passionate and active peace campaigner and advocated, albeit unsuccessfully, a peaceful end to American slavery before the outbreak of the American Civil War. In 1864, Abraham Lincoln himself appointed Elihu Burritt as Consul to Birmingham. Part of his role was to write annual reports for the State Department on economy, trade and industry around Birmingham and the Black Country.

4.   Walks in the Black Country and its Green Border-land

To write his reports for the state department, Elihu Burritt set about walking around the whole region. His reports eventually formed the basis of his 1868 book. The first line is the now famous, 'The Black Country, black by day and red by night, cannot be matched, for vast and varied production, by any other place of equal radius on the surface of the globe'. Black by day because of the continuous pall of black smoke that hung over it and red by night because of the illumination from all the forges and furnaces.

5.   Gracie Sheppard from Stourbridge

The Black Country Living Museum organised a competition to design a regional flag for the Black Country. In 2012 the winning design by 11-year-old Gracie Sheppard was officially adopted as a regional flag by the Flag Institute of Great Britain. The Black Country flag may be, and is, officially flown from public buildings and requires no special permission to do so.

6.   Chainmaking and glassmaking

The basic design and colours of the Black Country flag are based on Elihu Burritt's 'Black by day and Red by night' description of the area. The white section in the centre of the flag represents Stourbridge Red House Glass Cone. Appropriate really as the designer, Gracie Sheppard, is from Stourbridge. Industrial heritage is further represented by chains linking both sides of the flag. Since 2012, the Black Country flag has been proudly flown around the area and beyond.

7. Dudley, Sandwell, Walsall, and Wolverhampton

A sure-fire way to start an argument in the Black Country is to ask where its borders are. No two Black Country folk can ever seem to agree. The more modern view, and the view taken with this book, is that the Black Country includes the four metropolitan boroughs of Dudley, Sandwell, Walsall, and Wolverhampton. Most would agree that the Black Country is certainly contained within these areas but exactly where the borders are is open to much debate. Despite being our nearest neighbour, everyone will at least agree that Birmingham is most definitely not Black Country!

8. Coal, iron ore, and limestone

Whilst these are the essential ingredients for making iron, the Black Country was also rich in other mineral resources. Clay for brickmaking and also refractory or fireclay, used in the glass industry, was found here and also the fine sand used for castings. In fact, in a relatively small area the mineral resources necessary for the development of industry were found right here in the Black Country.

9. Silurian limestone fossils

Wrens Nest in Dudley is both a National Nature Reserve and a Site of Special Scientific Interest (SSI). Over 400 million years ago the area was under a Silurian sea, and the myriad of creatures that lived there have become preserved in the fossils that are found here. Many of these fossils are not found anywhere else in the world. Sir Roderick Murchison defined the Silurian time period and based his 1839 book, *The Silurian System*, on fossils found in Dudley.

10. River Stour and River Tame

The Black Country sits on the watershed of two major rivers, the Severn, and the Trent. Water from the River Stour flows into the Severn to the south west, and the River Tame into the Trent in the north east. In the Black Country, neither the Stour nor the Trent have ever been properly navigable, unlike the Severn in Shropshire which served the similarly industrialised area of Ironbridge. Little wonder then that the Black Country and Birmingham came to rely so heavily on the canal network.

Famous names

There were far too many well-known names in the Black Country to include them all here. Sadly, many of them have now disappeared. This section should stir a few memories of those that are included and perhaps even some that are not.

1. Established around 1868 which chain of tobacconists had branches throughout the Midlands?

2. The saying, 'If it was made out of metal, they made it' refers to which famous Bilston company?

3. Which butcher's shop in Brierley Hill went on to become a household name throughout the Black Country?

4. Which well-known name started with a 'Model Sausage Factory' in Tipton?

5. George Cadbury built a 'factory in a garden' at Bournville but which factory, sharing similar ideals, produced toffees in the Halesowen area?

6. In 1864, which major High Street bank opened its first branch office in Oldbury?

7. What well known range of kitchenware is associated with Mary Stevens Park in Stourbridge?

8. By what name did Bradley and Company of Bilston become famous for metalware and particularly ironing boards?

9. Which Oldbury tube manufacturer received a sample of the world's smallest tube from America and sent it back with an even smaller tube inside it?

10. Mander Brothers were well known paint and varnish manufacturers in Wolverhampton, but which National Trust property is the Mander family most associated with?

Question 7 – Mary Stevens Park

Answers – Section 2

1. **Alfred Preedy and Sons**

   Known locally as simply 'Preedys', these tobacconist shops had been a common sight in Black Country towns for over a century. As well as their own shops, Preedys were also wholesalers and had their own brands of tobacco and snuff. Their own pipe tobacco was advertised as, 'the smoke for men, not boys!' As well as tobacco products, the shops would stock a whole range of smoking paraphernalia including the popular briar pipes. Preedys is reminiscent of a time when the tobacconist's advice and skill would be sought by customers seeking their own blend or 'cut' of tobacco before the proliferation of mass market products such as cigarettes.

2. **Joseph Sankey and Sons Limited of Bilston**

   In 1854, Joseph Sankey was manufacturing blanks for the japanning industry. After setting up in Albert Street to produce holloware in 1867, the Bilston based company soon diversified into the developing automotive industry and patented the first all-steel wheel for motor cars in 1908. At its height, Sankeys produced a staggering range of metal items from domestic holloware to parts for jet engines during World War Two. In 1920, Sankeys became a subsidiary of Guest, Keen and Nettlefold, although it was not until much later that it became known as GKN Sankey. Once one of Bilston's biggest employers, a Morrisons Superstore now occupies part of the site.

3. **Marsh and Baxter Limited**

   Known simply as Marsh and Baxters, the Black Country chain of butchers had fifty-two shops at its peak and a massive bacon factory in Brierley Hill. By 1871, Alfred Marsh was curing and selling his own pork products from his Brierley Hill butcher's shop. It became Marsh and Baxter Limited when A. R. Baxter's meat processing factory in Birmingham was purchased. By 1978 the Brierley Hill factory was closed, and all of the shops sold.

4. Palethorpes

Palethorpes is another well-known name particularly for sausages but no longer produced in the Black Country. In 1896, Birmingham butcher Henry Palethorpe transferred his business to Tipton and claimed that his 'model sausage factory' was the largest in the world. It closed in 1968 when production was switched to Market Drayton where it continues to this day.

5. The Blue Bird Toffee Factory

Built between 1925 and 1927, the Blue Bird Toffee Factory at Hunnington near Halesowen was the vision of Birmingham toffee maker, Harry Vincent. Nestling at the foot of the Client Hills, Vincent's new factory was one of the largest and most modern in the world. As well as the factory, Vincent planned a model village along similar lines to Cadbury's Bournville with houses and amenities for his workers and their families. By 1998 production had switched to Hull but the former Administration Building on Bromsgrove Road is now Grade II listed.

6. Lloyds Bank

Lloyds Bank was founded in Birmingham by John Taylor, Sampson Lloyd, and their two sons in 1765. At this time, it was known as Taylor and Lloyds, becoming Lloyds and Company in 1852 when the connection with the Taylor family ended. It operated from Birmingham for nearly 100 years until opening a branch at Oldbury in 1864. It is said to have been the influence of Albright and Wilson, a large local chemical factory, which prompted the opening of the new branch. In 1865 it became Lloyds Banking Company Limited and is now simply known as Lloyds Bank.

7.   Judge Ware

Ernest Stevens had made his fortune in Judge kitchenware and holloware from his factory in Cradley Heath. He had lost his wife, Mary Stevens, in 1925 and set about making sizable public donations in her memory. One of these became Mary Stevens Park in Stourbridge after Ernest Stevens purchased Studley Court and grounds from the nuns who were running it as St Andrew's Convent School. It was presented to the people of Stourbridge in 1929 and Mary Stevens Park opened to the public in 1931. The magnificent park gates were also gifted by Ernest Stevens in memory of his wife.

8.   Beldray Limited

Beldray Limited can be traced back to 1872 when Walter S. Bradley purchased some land in Mount Pleasant Bilston and began to manufacture metal kitchenware known as hollowware. It was originally known as Bradley and Company Limited but later took on the well-known Beldray name. Beldray is an anagram of Bradley, but the story is that Walter's two young sons were playing with alphabet bricks, and he asked them to spell their names. One of his sons made a mistake and spelt his surname 'Beldray'. Walter liked it and renamed his company Beldray Limited. The company logo became a bell on a dray. The company closed in 2005 but the splendid 1930's style office building has been preserved and the name 'Beldray' lives on as it was bought out by another company.

9.   Accles and Pollock

The name Accles and Pollock was synonymous with tube manufacture in Oldbury. They produced tubing for bicycles, furniture and even the developing aero industry. In the 1930s, they were at the centre of Anglo-American engineering rivalry which would pass into Black Country legend. An American company proudly sent over a sample of tube claiming it to be the smallest in the world. Accles and Pollock returned the tube with one of their own even smaller tubes running through the middle of it.

10. Wightwick Manor in Wolverhampton

Arguably one of the finest examples in England of a house designed and furnished in Arts and Crafts style. The house was designed by architect Edward Ould for paint manufacturer, Theodore Mander. The house gives the appearance of a half-timbered Tudor residence but in fact is Victorian, being built in 1887 and enlarged in 1893. Ould specialised in 'Old English' style timber framing and tile hung walls which are a feature of Wightwick Manor.

World of work

The Black Country was not just about coal mining and heavy industry. The sheer variety of crafts and trades was staggering, although areas did tend to specialise such as Stourbridge for glass, Willenhall for locks, and Walsall for leather working. Many of these trades were highly skilled requiring precision craftmanship and in some cases artistic flair.

1. Which group of skilled glassmakers escaped religious persecution in France and eventually settled in the Stourbridge area?

2. What decorative art did the toymakers of Bilston perfect in the eighteenth century?

3. Where can the last working example of a traditional hand-made chain shop be found?

4. Willenhall had a nickname relating to a deformity caused by the lock making industry but what was it?

5. What was the principal occupation of the Lye Wasters who lived on common land to the east of The Lye itself?

6. Birmingham used to be at the centre of the gun trade but what did it rely on from the workshops of mainly Darlaston and Wednesbury?

7. Thousands of Black Country working families used to take part in which annual agricultural activity?

8. Many Walsall leather workers made high quality saddles but who made the metal items that make up a horse's harness?

9. What Coseley company was well known for manufacturing gas cookers and fires?

10. Before the invention of flushing toilets, it was common to have an earth closet in the back yard or garden, but who was paid to empty it?

Question 1 – Stourbridge glassmaking

Answers – Section 3

1.   The Huguenots

The Huguenots were French Protestants who fled to England in order to escape religious persecution. They came from the Lorraine area of north-eastern France and brought with them glassmaking skills. The reason they eventually settled in the Stourbridge area was the easy availability of the mineral resources needed for making glass. The abundance of coal and sand was important but in particular was the easy availability of heat proof fireclay essential for making furnace bricks and glass-melting pots.

2.   Bilston enamels

The industrial Black Country might seem a strange place for a fine decorative art to flourish but this was certainly the case in 18th century Bilston. The enamellers called themselves toymakers although toys in those day were not for children to play with. These 'toys' were the likes of decorative snuff boxes, scent boxes and patch boxes for beauty patches! Although intended for the well to do, Bilston enamels were generally on copper making them much more reasonably priced than enamelled gold or silver. In the case of the snuff boxes not to be sneezed at!

3.   Mushroom Green Chain Shop, Cradley Heath

Although the area was famous for production of industrial chain, cable chain for ship's anchors and the anchors themselves, a vast amount of smaller chain was made in backyard workshops such as the one preserved at Mushroom Green. The late Ron Moss, the Black Country Society, and the local authority in European Architectural Year (1975) ensured the preservation of the chain shop and restored it back to how it would have looked and operated when in use. Mushroom Green is now looked after by

Industrial Heritage Stronghold (IHS) who run regular Sunday afternoon chainmaking demonstrations in what is believed to be the last in situ traditional Black Country chain shop in existence.

4. Humpshire

Lock making in Willenhall can be traced back to the 16th century. It was very much a cottage industry with often whole families at work in small backyard workshops. It might be thought that lock making was a far healthier occupation than most in the black Country but not so. Lock makers often developed deformities including humps on their backs after spending their working lives bent over benches. This led to the nickname of 'Humpshire' or in the local dialect 'Umpshire' being applied to the town of Willenhall. At one time, some Willenhall pubs would have hollows carved out of the wooden backrests for customers with humps to enjoy their ale sitting upright.

5. Nailmakers

The Lye Wasters were mainly nailmakers and the area where they lived to the east of Lye was known locally as Mud City. A contemporary description of the living conditions from the time explains how many families had to live in little more than overcrowded mud huts with clay floors and thatched roofs. Industrialisation led to the demise of the handmade nail trade with the introduction of machine-made nails and particularly wire nails from around 1875 onwards.

6. Mainly gunlocks but barrels and other parts were also manufactured

Birmingham is known for its gun trade, but the various parts were often manufactured by sub-contractors, including those in Darlaston and Wednesbury. Gunlocks (firing mechanisms) together with barrels and other components used in the manufacture of firearms were supplied to the Birmingham gunmakers. In 1813 an Act of Parliament established Birmingham's own Proof House, reflecting the importance of the trade at that time. An overcharged proof load would be fired through the gun barrels in order to test them. The Proof House in Banbury Street is now a listed building.

7. Hop picking

Despite being such a highly industrialised area, for many families hop picking was an important annual activity in September and October. For most working folk this would be the only break they would get, swapping the smoke and grime of the Black Country for the hopyards of rural Worcestershire, Herefordshire, and Shropshire. Even so, it was hard work and often the living conditions on the farms were harsh. Men, women, and children were on piecework rates for picking hops meaning they were only paid for what they picked.

8. The loriners

Loriners arrived in the Walsall area for much the same reasons as industry flourished in other parts of the Black Country. They needed the mineral resources which were in plentiful supply to be able to manufacture the metal parts of a horse's harness which is known as lorinery. Once loriners established themselves it made sense for leather workers and particularly saddle makers to follow suit. Walsall was, and still is, known worldwide for its high-quality leather working industry.

9. Cannon Industries

Known locally as simply 'The Cannon', it was originally The Cannon Foundry when it opened in 1826 and later Cannon Industries. Cannon became well-known for household ironmongery known as holloware. By the early 1900s they had diversified into gas cookers and gas fires. Cannon went on to become a leading manufacturer of gas appliances and gas fires. A major local employer, Cannon moved to Stoke-on-Trent in 1993.

10. **The night soil men**

In the days before proper sanitation overcrowded households could find themselves having to share a very basic toilet in the yard or back garden. A simple bucket or earth closet would often be used to collect the waste but then it had to be emptied. This is where the night soil men came in. They were paid to go from house to house emptying the human waste onto a cart. The job was considered so horrible that they were only allowed to work during the hours of darkness.

Ironmaking and mining

Without mining and ironmaking, it is difficult to see how the Black Country would have developed as such a major industrialised area. The region had all the essential mineral resources for heavy industry together with clay suitable for brick making and the fine sand necessary for castings.

1. The huge blast furnace at Bilston Steel Works had a girl's name but what was it?

2. When was it made illegal for girls, women, or boys under ten to work underground in the mines?

   a. 1842

   b. 1852

   c. 1862

   d. 1872

3. Who was the first person to smelt iron using pit-coal or sea-coal?

4. The Darby family is associated with Ironbridge but where was Abraham Darby I born?

5. Traditionally, who should relight a blast furnace to avoid it going out?

6. What was the name of the last deep coal mine to close in the Black Country?

7. The Black Country sits on a seam of South Staffordshire coal known as 'the thick', but just how thick was this seam?

8. If you were employed at 'the Earl's' in Brierley Hill, where would you be working?

9. The Black Country had abundant quantities of limestone but what was its purpose in the smelting of iron?

10. What was the Pillar and Stall technique used for?

Question 9 - Wren's Nest limestone (Copyright Ashley Dace)

Answers – Section 4

1. **Elisabeth**

    In 1920 Stewarts and Lloyds took over Bilston Steel Works from the Hickman family who had acquired it in 1866. In 1954, a new blast furnace replaced three existing ones and became affectionately known as Elisabeth (spelt with an 's'), after the daughter of the company chairman, and not the young Queen Elizabeth (spelt with a 'z'). Elisabeth was the last remaining blast furnace in the Black Country, and she was demolished in 1980.

2. **a. 1842**

    Prior to The Mines and Collieries Act of 1842 it was common for women, girls, and boys under the age of ten to work underground in the mines. Younger children, typically from the age of about six, were often employed as 'trappers' for up to 12 hours in a shift. Their job would be to open and close trap doors in the dark to allow the passage of coal tubs. In fact, they were actually controlling the air flow through the mine. A very responsible job for a young child.

3. **Dud Dudley**

    Dud Dudley was one of eleven illegitimate children fathered by Edward Sutton, 5th Baron Dudley, and his mistress, Elizabeth Tomlinson, who was described as a 'lewd and infamous woman'. Dud Dudley had an Oxford education paid for by his father and set about improving the iron making process using coal instead of charcoal. He had his father take out a patent in 1620 for smelting iron using what he called 'sea coals' or 'pit coals' in furnaces with bellows. This required coal with the impurities removed which is coke. Never entirely successful with his furnaces and forges, the English Civil War interrupted his ironmaking activities when he became a Royalist Colonel. Dud Dudley is remembered for his 1665 book, *Metallum Martis*, which records his use of coal in the ironmaking process.

4. Woodsetton, on the Sedgley side of Wrens Nest

The Darby family dynasty of Coalbrookdale in Shropshire are generally credited with the successful smelting of iron using coke rather than charcoal. Abraham Darby I not only originated from the Black Country but also the same area where Dud Dudley was making iron using a form of coke. Born in 1678, he would have been well aware of the process used by Dud Dudley and also his 1665 book, *Metallum Martis*. Interestingly, Abraham Darby's family can be traced back to Edward Sutton and Elizabeth Tomlinson, the parents of Dud Dudley himself.

5. A young girl

There is superstition around the naming and lighting of blast furnaces in the Black Country. Traditionally, if a blast furnace was not lit by a young girl, it would go out. The last blast furnace in the Black Country at Stewarts and Lloyds was first lit by Elisabeth, the young daughter of the company chairman. Local legend has it that after a relining, a workman tried to light the furnace but to no avail until a little girl was found to do the job!

6. Baggeridge Colliery

Baggeridge Colliery at Gospel End near Sedgley was the last deep coal mine in the Black Country. It reached full production in 1912 and at its peak produced around 10,000 tons of coal per week and employed approximately 2,000 people. Baggeridge was nationalised in 1947 but closed in 1968 when the cost of extracting the coal became too expensive. The area where Baggeridge Colliery stood is now a country park which was opened by Princess Anne in 1983. Many believe that the closing of Baggeridge Colliery in 1968 signalled the end of the old industrial Black Country.

7. The thirty-foot or ten-yard coal seam

Much of the Black Country lies on the South Staffordshire Coalfield. Traditionally though, the old Black Country consists of the area around the famous thirty-foot or ten-yard coal seam. This is the thickest seam of coal to be found in Britain. Hence it is known locally as the 'thick'. Miners of old recognised different seams within the thick coal and indeed there were other workable seams of coal present throughout the Black Country.

8. Round Oak Steel Works

It was said that if you had a job at 'the Earl's' in Brierley Hill, you had a job for life. Sadly, like so much of the industry in the Black Country, this ultimately proved not to be the case. Round Oak was established in 1857 as a major part of Lord (later Earl) Dudley's commercial interests. At the height of production, it employed around 3,500 people. Round Oak Steel Works finally closed in 1982 marking the end of an era for Brierley Hill.

9. Limestone acted as a flux to remove impurities

The principal mineral resources needed for making iron are iron ore, coke (derived from coal), and limestone. These resources were all abundant in the Black Country. Although many industries and processes made use of limestone, it was employed particularly as a flux to remove impurities in the ironmaking process. In a blast furnace, the limestone and impurities form slag which floats to the surface and is drawn off leaving the molten iron.

10. Mining

The Pillar and Stall method is also known by several other names including Pillar and Room. It is a technique used in mining. A series of stalls or rooms are dug out leaving pillars to support the roof. Where the coal seams and limestone layers were thick enough, this method of mining was often used in the Black Country.

Industrial steam power

It was steam power that really drove the Industrial Revolution and it started right here in the Black Country with Thomas Newcomen's atmospheric steam engine. With later improvements by James Watt and his partnership with Mathew Boulton, steam engines transformed the Industrial Revolution.

1. In which year did Thomas Newcomen erect the world's first practical atmospheric steam engine at Tipton?

    a. 1702

    b. 1712

    c. 1722

    d. 1732

2. What were Newcomen's first and subsequent atmospheric steam engines designed to do?

3. What alternative name did Newcomen engines have which means something quite different today?

4. The only full-sized steam powered replica of Newcomen's original engine can be seen where?

5. When Mathew Boulton, James Watt, and their sons established the world's first steam engine manufactory in Smethwick, what did they call it?

6.   John Wilkinson's boring machines proved ideal for boring cylinders for steam engines but what were they originally designed to manufacture?

7.   What is the name of the historic mine pumping engine house pictured?

8.   James Watt patented an idea by employee, William Murdoch, to turn the vertical motion of a beam engine into circular motion and named it after which celestial bodies?

9.   What is the name of the oldest working steam engine in the world designed by James Watt and now preserved at Thinktank in Birmingham?

10. Widely regarded as the largest steam engine in the Black Country, the blast furnace blowing engine used by M. & W. Grazebrook of Netherton can now be found in which unlikely location?

Question 7 – (Tina Cordon CC BY-SA 3.0)

Answers – Section 5

1. **b. 1712**

   Thomas Newcomen and his partner, John Calley, erected the world's first successful steam engine in Tipton, although the exact location is still subject to speculation. A contemporary engraving by Thomas Barney in 1719 calls it 'The steam engine near Dudley Castle'. This was an atmospheric steam engine with a single large cylinder and piston operating a massive hinged wooden beam. It was powered by a low-pressure boiler as it would be the early 19th century before high pressure steam could be safely controlled. Weight alone moved the piston to the top of the cylinder with the gap left behind being filled with steam. Cold water was sprayed in condensing the steam and creating a vacuum. Atmospheric pressure then forced the piston down again producing the power. The engine was capable of about twelve complete cycles per minute.

2. **Pump water out of mines**

   Flooding in mines was a national problem but especially here in the Black Country. Prior to Newcomen's success with his atmospheric steam engine, various methods of expelling the water from deep underground had all proved largely ineffective. His other great innovation was to attach a series of 10-gallon pumps to the large wooden beam on the opposite end to the cylinder. These would be linked by rods and go deep into the mine to remove the flood water. Newcomen's engines could reliably remove about 120 gallons per minute.

3. **Fire engines**

   Newcomen engines were known as 'fire engines'. They were relatively inefficient using vast quantities of coal and belching out thick black smoke. This alone would be enough to justify the name but there might be another explanation. Thomas Savery held a patent for 'fire engines' and pumping water from mines by the 'impellent force of fire'. Although Savery's pump had serious limitations, Newcomen found it advantageous to partner with Savery for the use of his extended patent.

4. The Black Country Living Museum

Nothing remains of Newcomen's original 1712 engine apart from an engraving made in 1719 by Thomas Barney. Over ten years of detailed research culminated in the building of the world's only full-size steam powered Newcomen engine at the Black Country Living Museum in 1986. It is particularly significant as the original 1712 engine is thought to have been erected at the Coneygree Coal Mine in Tipton, no more than a mile or so from the museum site.

5. The Soho Foundry

Up until 1794, Mathew Boulton and James Watt had been relying on suppliers to build their steam engines. Together with their sons, Mathew Robinson Boulton, James Watt Junior and Gregory Watt, they formed a partnership to build a new steam engine works. In 1796 the Soho Foundry opened in Smethwick. This was the first purpose-built steam engine works in the world. There are plans to preserve this very important industrial archaeology site for the future.

6. Military cannons

John 'Iron Mad' Wilkinson had ironworks in Wales and Shropshire as well as Bradley in the Black Country. He initially developed his innovative 'boring bar' to accurately bore military cannons. Wilkinson was able to adapt his existing technology to produce new machines capable of accurately boring cylinders for the steam engines of Boulton and Watt. Although never a partner,

Wilkinson was crucial to the early success of the Boulton Watt steam engines that powered the industrial revolution.

7.   Cobbs Engine House and Chimney

Cobbs Engine House and Chimney (Windmill End Pumping Station) is a Grade II listed building and Scheduled Ancient Monument in the Bumble Hole and Warrens Hall nature reserves. It is said to be named after a man called Cobb who once farmed the land. Built around 1831, its purpose was to pump water from local mines into the adjacent canal. It housed a Watt type beam engine capable of pumping around 367,000 gallons of water per day from a 525 feet (160 metre) deep shaft. As well as being one of the few remaining engine houses in the Black Country, it is the earliest surviving example.

8.   Sun and planet gear

Although patented by James Watt it was employee, William Murdoch, who came up with the idea of the sun and planet gear. It used two rotating gears to turn vertical motion from a steam engine into circular motion to power machinery. It solved an existing problem with a patent taken out by James Pickard to use a simple crank and flywheel to do the same job. Although an employee at the time, William Murdoch would later become a partner with Boulton and Watt. William Murdoch is perhaps best remembered for the development of gas lighting.

9.   The Smethwick Engine

Designed by James Watt, the Smethwick Engine started work in 1779 and was used to pump water back up a series of locks on the Birmingham Canal Old Main Line at Smethwick. Water would travel down the locks as boats passed through and needed to be pumped back up. This engine was the first in the world to use both atmospheric pressure together with the expansive force of steam. This would set the design standard for years to come. The

Smethwick Engine is preserved at Birmingham's Thinktank and is the oldest working steam engine in the world.

10. **Dartmouth Circus roundabout, Birmingham**

The Grazebrook Engine was built to a design by James Watt in 1817 and is regarded as having been the largest steam engine in the Black Country. It was used as a 'blowing engine' to force air into two blast furnaces to obtain the high temperature necessary to smelt iron. It was in regular use up until 1912 at the Netherton works of M. & W. Grazebrook. It was then kept in full working order until 1964 when it was acquired by the Birmingham Science Museum who have relocated it to Dartmouth Circus roundabout.

Hard times

There can be no denying that life was hard for working people in the industrial Black Country, with large families often living in substandard and overcrowded accommodation. Pollution, industrial accidents, disease, lack of proper sanitation, and poor health care all took their toll. In 1841, the average age of death in Dudley was 16 years and 7 months with many children not surviving childbirth or reaching adulthood. In 1852 it was reported that Dudley was the most unhealthy place in the country.

1. Who led the women chainmakers of Cradley Heath out on strike in 1910 when employers refused to pay the legal minimum wage?

2. The oldest woman chainmaker to go on strike in 1910 was Patience Round, but how old was she at the time?

    a. 59

    b. 69

    c. 79

    d. 89

3. Why did Lucy Woodall become something of a celebrity in her later years?

4. How were apprentice nailmakers often punished for shoddy work or insolence?

5. What was the so-called murder bottle used for?

6. What year was the Workhouse system abolished by Parliament?

    a. 1910

    b. 1920

    c. 1930

    d. 1940

7. What were the middlemen called who often cheated home workers in the nail and chainmaking industries?

8. What did the truck system of payment involve?

9. Dudley Guest Hospital was originally built to house workers who had suffered from what?

10. What was the terrible 'blue death' that killed thousands in the Black Country?

Question 9 – Dudley Guest Hospital

Answers – Section 6

1. **Mary Reid Macarthur**

   In 1910 the Chain Trade Board set a minimum wage of 2½d per hour. This mainly affected women chainmakers who were working from home on peacework rates that were only half the minimum wage. When local employers in the Black Country refused to pay the new rate Mary Macarthur of the National Federation of Women Workers (NFWW) brought them out on strike. The strike lasted approximately ten weeks, involving around 800 women at its height. Under the charismatic leadership of Mary Macarthur, the women won an outright victory and struck a resounding blow for the principles of both women's rights and a national minimum wage.

2. **c. 79**

   The publicity campaign mounted by Mary Macarthur during the chainmaking women's strike of 1910 was quite remarkable. She used all of the media available to her in order to publicise the plight of the women chainmakers. She had a group of the oldest women chainmakers photographed for the newspapers in their Sunday best with some of them wearing chains around their necks. Patience Round was the oldest at 79 in 1910 and still a full-time chainmaker. She liked to talk about her life and her story appeared in the newspapers of the day. After the strike Patience Round became something of a local celebrity and remarkably lived to be 103!

3. **She was last of the hand-hammered women chainmakers**

   Lucy Woodall was the last of her kind. Born in 1899, she had started work at the forge aged fourteen making hand-hammered chain for 4 shillings (20p) a week. The hours were long too, and Lucy worked a twelve-hour day when she started. She retired in

1969 but returned to the anvil part-time and continued working up until 1973. A local celebrity in her later life, Lucy Woodall passed away in 1979 just shy of her eightieth birthday.

4. **An ear would be nailed to the bench**

Of all the Black Country trades, nailmakers had a particularly tough time of it. No wonder perhaps that apprentice nailmakers were subjected to such a punishment for shoddy work or insolence. Nailmaking was very often a whole family affair with a forge in the backyard often rented along with a basic cottage. Nailmakers were only paid for what they made on a piecework basis. Appalling conditions, low pay and the threat of cheap imports and machine-made nails led to deprivation, starvation, and riots for many nailmakers.

5. **Feeding babies**

The so called 'murder bottles' were a Victorian attempt to encourage babies to feed themselves. With quaint names such as 'Little Cherub' and 'Mummies Darling' they consisted of a banjo shaped bottle with a long rubber tube leading to a teat for the baby to suck on. They were almost impossible to clean properly inevitably leading to the build-up of deadly bacteria. They were condemned by doctors, but many mothers followed Mrs Beaton's advice that the teats did not really need washing for two or three weeks anyway!

6. **c. 1930**

On the 1st of April 1930, the Local Government Act passed the previous year effectively abolished the system of workhouses and Boards of Guardians. This system dated as far back as the Poor Law Amendment Act of 1834, which was known as the 'new poor law'. Responsibilities in 1930 were passed over to local authorities. Many former workhouses became Public Assistance Institutions and continued to provide accommodation for elderly people, the disabled, unmarried mothers and the homeless. They were no longer called workhouses and had a less strict regime, but even so improvements came about gradually over subsequent decades.

7. Foggers

Nailmaking was big business in the Black Country around 1820 when it is estimated there was something like 50,000 nailmakers in major centres such as Halesowen, Old Hill, The Lye, Dudley, Gornal and Sedgley. It was mainly a cottage industry employing men, women, and children as either outworkers for the nail masters, or else they were at the mercy of middlemen called 'foggers'. The 'foggers' were notoriously corrupt and would often cheat the nailmakers with doctored weighing scales and payment in kind rather than coin of the realm.

8. Payment in kind

Truck was the system of paying for labour or goods in kind rather than coin of the realm. This was common where middlemen in the nailmaking, chainmaking or mining industries operated between the workers and the employers. Workers were often coerced into accepting inferior and expensive goods using 'tommy notes' or tokens from shops run by the middlemen. Not only that, but workers would be encouraged to exchange 'beer tokens' in beerhouses run by the same middlemen. The truck system had been banned by Act of Parliament in 1831, but still carried on more or less unabated for many years in the Black Country.

9. Blindness

In 1860, the newly created Earl of Dudley inaugurated 'The Dudley Asylum for the Blind'. This was built to accommodate twenty-six workers who had been blinded in the Earl's limestone and coal mines together with their families. There was also a school, chapel, and medical facilities on site. The project failed as the 'almshouses' were not appreciated by the blinded men who preferred the freedom of living with their families in their own homes. The asylum became the Dudley Guest Hospital in 1871. Although Lord Dudley put a great deal of money into the new hospital it was named after the wealthy local industrialist Joseph Guest who had also made a significant contribution.

10. Cholera

It was nicknamed the Blue Death because the severe diarrhea and dehydration caused by Cholera would often turn the bodies a bluish colour. The disease spread rapidly through contaminated water and killed thousands in the Black Country. Particularly severe epidemics occurred in 1832 and 1849 with densely populated areas such as Bilston being particularly badly hit.

That's entertainment

The Black Country has been the birthplace of a surprising number of film stars and artists over many years. In more recent times the world of acting includes Julie Walters, Liza Goddard, and Frances Barber. Comedians and writers include Meera Syal, Lenny Henry and Frank Skinner. From the world of music there is Robert Plant and Noddy Holder whilst television presenters include Sue Lawley and Bill Odie. There are many others, but this quiz is concerned with days gone by.

1. Which West Bromwich born actress starred in the 1935 movie, *The 39 Steps,* with Robert Donat?

2. Born in The Lye, who became the youngest actor to receive a knighthood in 1941?

3. Birmingham based Oscar Deutsch, founder of the Odeon cinema chain built his first cinema where?

4. What was the name of the earlier theatre on the site of the Dudley Hippodrome?

5. Who wrote the popular Great War marching song, *It's a Long way to Tipperary?*

6. Captain Sydney Clift of the Royal Flying Core was best known for what?

7. A Bilston man wrote the popular poems *Drake's Drum* and *The Fighting Temeraire* but who was he?

8. Who was the Dudley born comedian and star of pantomime famous for his funny walks?

9. What musical instrument was manufactured in the Black Country and particularly around Rowley Regis?

10. Who was the young performer who came to Dudley in 1906 with Will Murray's Casey's Court and later became a major Hollywood star?

Actor of Stage and Screen
Born Lye Cross House 1893
Died 1964 in New York

He was knighted for his
Stage career in 1934 before
finding critical acclaim
in such films as 'The Hunchback of
Notre Dame (1939) and The Ghost of
Come (1935) and The
Frankenstein (19...
others...

Question 2 – Lye memorial to famous actor

Answers – Section 7

1. Madeleine Carroll

The 39 Steps is a classic 1935 film loosely based on John Buchan's 1915 novel of the same name directed by Alfred Hitchcock. It starred Robert Donat as Richard Hannay and Madeleine Carroll as Pamela. She was born in Herbert Street West Bromwich in 1906 and moved to nearby Jesson Street with her parents in 1912. She went on to become a major British and Hollywood film star and in her movie career she made over forty films. In later life she became one of the first ambassadors for UNICEF working for displaced and orphaned children after World War Two.

2. Cedric Hardwicke

Cedric Webster Hardwicke was born at Lye Cross House in 1893. After failing to qualify as a medical doctor he took up acting. Following a spell in the First World War his acting career began to take off. He graduated to the London stage where several defining roles led to him being awarded a knighthood by King George V in 1934. Aged just forty-one Cedric Hardwicke was then the youngest actor to have achieved such recognition. He went on to become a celebrated Hollywood film actor.

3. Brierley Hill

Oscar Deutsch was born in 1893 at Balsall Heath in Birmingham but he built his first cinema in the Black Country. This was the Picture House in Brierley Hill which opened in 1928. Always abreast with new technology, he converted it from silent to sound in 1930 in order to show the new 'talking pictures'. The name Odeon might never have come about as Oscar Deutsch had planned another Picture House for Perry Barr but there was an existing cinema with the same name. Fellow investor Mel Mindelsohn had seen the name Odeon in Tunisia which coincidentally contained Oscar's initials. The Odeon name would later acquire the acronym 'Oscar Deutsch Entertains Our Nation'.

4. **Dudley Opera House**

The Dudley Opera House on Castle Hill opened its doors in September 1899. It was built to hold around 2,000 patrons in opulent splendour with its domed ceiling and fine decor. It was even lit by electric lights rather than gas. A young performer in 1908 was Arthur Stanley Jefferson. He would later achieve worldwide fame as Stan Laurel. Laurel and Hardy would later appear at the Hippodrome on the same site. Disaster befell the Opera House in the early morning of the 1st of November 1936. A fire had broken out which was to destroy the building despite the best efforts of the fire brigade. The Dudley Hippodrome opened as the replacement theatre in 1938.

5. **Jack Judge**

Born John Thomas Judge at Oldbury in 1872, he was known to all as Jack. His famous song came about in 1912 when he was booked to perform at the Grand Theatre in Stalybridge just outside Manchester. A favourite trick between performances was to bet that he could pen a new song overnight and perform it the next day. That song to win his five-shilling bet was *It's a long way to Tipperary*. The title was later changed to *It's a long, long way to Tipperary* and became one of the most popular First World War marching songs.

6. **Clifton Cinemas**

Centred around the Black Country and Birmingham, Sidney Clift was involved with the building and acquisition of cinemas in the 1920s and 1930s. An association with theatre proprietor Leon Salberg led to the formation of Cinema Accessories Limited in 1934, which managed the Clifton chain of cinemas. Sydney Clift had served in the Royal Flying Core (RFC) during the First World War where he earned the rank of captain. The last Clifton Cinema to be built was at Coseley in 1939, just before the start of the Second World War. At its peak the chain had thirty six cinemas. Captain Sydney Clift would later become Sir Sydney Clift.

7. Sir Henry Newbolt

Henry Newbolt (1862 – 1938) was born in Bilston. His father was the Reverend Henry Francis Newbolt of St Mary's Church. The young Henry Newbolt won a scholarship to Oxford, and after becoming a Barrister was later knighted. Many of his famous poems such as *Drake's Drum* and *The Fighting Temeraire* related to the sea. Although not a naval man himself, his grandfather on his father's side had been a Royal Navy captain. His most famous poem *Vitai Lampada* (Torch of Life) is about a schoolboy cricketer who becomes a soldier and urges his comrades to 'play the game'.

8. Billy Dainty

Billy Dainty (1927 – 1986) was born in Wolverhampton Street, Dudley. The young Billy was encouraged to take dancing lessons and became one of the Betty Fox Babes in Birmingham. After the family had moved to London, he won a scholarship to RADA and never looked back. Billy Dainty is best remembered particularly for his silly walks, comic dance routines and roles as a pantomime dame. Billy Dainty made the transition from music hall to television and appeared on Royal Variety Performances and Sunday Night at the London Palladium.

9. Jew's Harp

The Jew's Harp is an instrument shaped a bit like a keyhole with a thin strip of metal down the middle. It is played with a combination of twanging the metal strip with a finger whilst modulating the sound with the mouth. In the earlier part of the

19th century production of Jew's Harps for supply around the world was centred in the Black Country and particularly Rowley Regis. Demand and the need for mass production would see this once cottage industry transferring to the workshops of Birmingham.

10. Charlie Chaplin

The young Charlie Chaplin joined Will Murray's Casey's Court in 1906. It is possible that the Dudley Opera House saw one of his earliest appearances in this show. Chaplin later joined the Fred Karno Company which also played in the Black Country. When the troupe went to America, two of the young players would make names for themselves in Hollywood. One was Charlie Chaplin, and the other was Arthur Stanley Jefferson who would later be known as Stan Laurel of Laurel and Hardy fame.

Sporting life

Sport has always played an important part in the Black Country. Whether that be playing or watching it has long provided a welcome release from the daily grind. Companies often had their own leisure facilities for workers, but with the demise of local industry many of these former sports grounds have also been lost.

1. Champion prizefighter William Perry, 'The Tipton Slasher', had his headquarters in which Tipton pub?

2. Dudley Wood Stadium was home to which famous club?

3. The wife of Dudley's Dr Douglas Little was better known as which sportswoman?

4. Born in 1873 and from Smethwick, who is considered by many to have been England's finest test bowler?

5. Which Wolverhampton Wanderers player was the first footballer to win 100 caps for England?

6. Until the publication of the Marquis of Queensbury rules in 1867, how long did a bare-knuckle prizefighting round last in the 19th century?

7. Which famous Black Country sportsman was once a member of his school Morris Dancing team?

8. Which well-known football club was originally formed in 1878 by a group of young workers from the George Salter & Company factory?

9. Who was the greatest Victorian spring jumper, a forgotten sport often using weights to achieve incredible standing jumps?

10. Which local football ground was the venue for cycle racing in the late 19th century?

Question 1 – The Tipton Slasher

Answers – Section 8

1. The Fountain Inn

William Perry (1819 – 1880) was born in Tipton and grew up to become the legendary 'Tipton Slasher', a champion prize fighter. Perry honed his fighting skills from a young age working on the narrow boats. Queuing for the locks would often result in fights for position and Perry never lost. By 1850 he had fought his way up for a chance at the title and defeated Tom Paddock to become the Champion of England. He would hold this title (with a disputed break between 1851 and 1853) for seven years until the now overweight and unfit Tipton Slasher lost to Tom Sayers. Perry had made his headquarters at The Fountain Inn, Owen Street, and a bronze statue of the Tipton Slasher now stands proudly opposite in Coronation Gardens.

2. Cradley Heathens motorcycle speedway team

The first Cradley Heath speedway team was formed in 1947 and took on a disused site at Dudley Wood. Despite some initial success speedway ended at Dudley Wood in 1952. Speedway began again in 1960 when the Cradley Heathens reformed. The big change in fortunes came in 1965 with the formation of the British League. The end of speedway in Cradley Heath came in 1995 when the land was sold off for housing. The supporters cry of 'Ommer em Cradley' (hammer them) would no longer be heard at Dudley Wood.

3. Dorothy Round

Dorothy Edith Round (1909 – 1982) was born in Dudley. She showed a natural gift for tennis playing against her three brothers and playing for Dudley Girls' High School. During her tennis career she won the Wimbledon ladies' singles championship in both 1934 and 1937. She married Dr Douglas Leigh Little at the

Wesley Methodist Church in Dudley on September 2nd, 1937. She made her last appearance at Wimbledon in 1939. In 2013 a commemorative statue was unveiled in Dudley's Priory Park by her daughter.

4. **Sidney Francis Barnes**

Born in Smethwick, Sydney Francis Barnes (1873 – 1967) was considered by his peers to have been the best bowler they had ever seen. His world-class reputation was established during the Second Test against Australia in 1902 when he took 13 wickets. Over seven tests against South Africa Barnes took 83 wickets and broke several records. The Wisden Cricketer's Almanac for 1910 named Sydney Francis Barnes as one of the cricketers of the year. In 1963 Wisden named him as one of the six giants of the Wisden century.

5. **Billy Wright**

Billy Wright was born in Ironbridge, Shropshire and encouraged by one of his teachers he applied for a trial at Wolverhampton Wanderers aged 14. Initially feeling he was not tall enough, Wright was nevertheless kept on to help the ground staff! He played his debut game for Wolves in 1939. After the Second World War Wright's career took off playing for both Wolves and England. In 1959 he became the first player to be awarded 100 international caps for England. A memorial statue now stands outside the Molineux Stadium's Billy Wright stand, at the club where he spent his entire playing career.

6. **Until one or other of the pugilists got knocked down**

Up until 1743 bare-knuckle boxing was both illegal and completely unregulated. There were no rounds and fights would continue until one of the opponents was defeated. In 1743 prizefighter Jack Broughton introduced the first set of rules. A round would last until a fighter was knocked down. He would then have thirty seconds to recover and face his opponent. With the introduction of the London Prize Ring Rules in 1838, the thirty second recovery remained after a knock down but a further eight seconds was added for the fighter to get to the centre of the ring. In 1867 the Marquess of Queensbury rules called for gloved fights and brought in the familiar three-minute rounds with a ten second count after a knock down, although bare-knuckle fights still continued.

7. Duncan Edwards

Arguably England's greatest ever footballer and tragically killed as a result of the 1958 Munich Air Disaster, Duncan Edwards was born and went to school in Dudley. Even as a pupil at Priory Primary School Duncan was head and shoulders above his classmates both in height and skill with a football. Whilst at Wolverhampton Street Secondary School in Dudley Duncan was playing for the Dudley Schools area team, Birmingham and Worcestershire district teams and the England School team. Football was clearly not his only skill as alongside football he also represented his school at Morris Dancing! There is a museum dedicated to Duncan Edwards in Castle Street, Dudley.

8. West Bromwich Albion

The club was founded in 1878 although not called West Bromwich Albion at that time. The story goes that a group of young workers from the spring works of George Salter and Company were looking for a sport to play in the winter after the cricket season had ended and chose football. Initially, they were called the West Bromwich Strollers but soon changed the name to West Bromwich Albion. The distinctive 'boing boing' chant unfortunately has nothing to do with the lads from Salter's Spring Works, as it only originated in the early 1990s.

9. Joe Darby

Spring Jumping was a popular sport in the Victorian period and young Joseph Darby from Windmill End Netherton excelled at it. He became known locally as 'Joesy the Jumper'. Spring Jumping involved jumping forwards or backwards from a standing start with or without the addition of dumbbells held in each hand and released at the right moment. He held numerous official jumping records along with performing amazing tricks such as jumping from a tumbler filled with water and clearing twelve chairs without spilling a drop. Having defeated American G. W. Hamilton, champion of the world, Joe Darby took this title for himself.

10. The Molineux Stadium

The name comes from the former Molineux Hotel which is now home to the Wolverhampton City Archives and looks down over the football ground. The large house became a hotel in 1871 and the extensive park was used for all sorts of leisure activities and sports. Bicycle races proved particularly popular drawing crowds of up to 20,000 people. By 1889 the grounds were being used by a local football club, Wolverhampton Wanderers.

Church and religion

Church and chapel played an important part in the lives of local communities. Apart from regular Sunday services, congregations would come together for important events such as marriages, christenings, and funerals. Children would attend Sunday School, which prior to compulsory education which came in gradually from 1870 onwards, might have been the only formal education they received. The highlight of the year for children was usually the Sunday School outing, and regular social events for the whole congregation were a common feature, often resulting in marriages and christenings!

1.   Which side destroyed Saint Edmund's Church in Dudley, known locally as 'bottom church', during the English Civil War?

2.   Known locally as 'top church' in Dudley what is its correct name?

3.   What denomination were the Gornal Ranters who originally met in the back room of the Chapel House pub until they acquired their own place of worship in 1841?

4.   William Booth was living in Walsall with his family in 1863 and later went on to found what organisation in London?

5.   Where in Halesowen could White Canons once be found?

6.   The oldest man-made structure in Walsall is the crypt of which church?

7.   One of the first Quaker Meeting Houses in the country, built shortly after the Act of Toleration in May 1689, can be found where?

8.   Who nearly lost his life in 1743 after preaching Methodism in Wednesbury causing riots to break out?

9.   What was the biblical name of the friendly society which required all members to sign the pledge and be teetotal before joining?

10. Who was the Anglo-Saxon Lady who endowed a monastery in 994 which became St Peter's Collegiate Church in Wolverhampton?

Question 3 – Chapel House Pub

Answers – Section 9

1. The Royalists

In April to May 1646 a second English Civil War siege took place at Dudley Castle. The castle was a Royalist stronghold and Colonel Leveson, the commander, seemed determined to hold out against the Parliamentarian forces under Sir William Brereton. To this end Leveson had buildings around the castle destroyed, including the Church of St Edmund (bottom church), in order to avoid them being used by the enemy. In the event, Dudley Castle was surrendered without a fight on the 13th of May 1646. The Church of St Edmund was rebuilt in 1724.

2. The Church of St Thomas and St Luke

At the other end of the ancient town of Dudley from the Church of St Edmund lies the Church of St Thomas and St Luke, known locally as 'top church'. The original medieval church was replaced in the early 19th century but part of what was probably the original crypt remains. The church is Grade II listed, not the least for its structural ironwork instead of wood reflecting the industrial heritage of the Black Country.

3. Primitive Methodists

The Primitive Methodists were a 19th century working class movement which had broken away from Wesleyan Methodism. Encouraged by the Darlaston Circuit, a group known as the Gornal Ranters began meeting in each other's homes from around 1820. Later, they were allowed to meet in the back room of a pub which became known as the Chapel House. By 1841, they were able to acquire their own place of worship in nearby Lake Street. The name of the pub was changed to the Miner's Arms but continued to be called the Chapel House by Gornal folk. The pub is once again called by its original 1835 name of the Chapel House.

4. **The Salvation Army**

In 1863 William Booth (later General) was living with his wife and children at 5, Hatherton Street, Walsall. He ran a mission and took to marching through the slum areas of Walsall gathering people to be addressed from waggons by reformed reprobates. These were often characters much given to fighting, drinking and profanity before they were converted by Booth and formed into 'Halleluiah Bands'. Booth later took these ideas to the East End of London and formed the Christian Mission. In 1878, the Christian Mission was renamed the Salvation Army.

5. **Halesowen Abbey**

The Manor of Hales was given to Peter des Roches, Bishop of Winchester, in 1214 to build a 'religious house'. The Abbey was officially established in 1218 and dedicated to the Virgin and St John the Evangelist. Halesowen Abbey was occupied by Premonstratensian Canons for over 300 years. They were known as White Canons because of the undyed habits that they wore. Dissolution under Henry VIII came in 1538 and Halesowen Abbey was partly demolished two years later.

6. **St Matthews Church**

St Matthews sits high above Walsall and looks out over the High Street and the town as it has done for hundreds of years. In common with most ancient churches, it has been added to and restored over the years. It is the inner room of the crypt which has the reputation of being the oldest man-made structure in Walsall. There are two 12th century lancet windows and the remains of a Norman doorway. This used to lead to a stairway up to the chancel above.

7. Stourbridge

Before the Act of Toleration in 1689 a group of Quakers or Friends were meeting discreetly in each other's houses. Once the Act came into force, the Friends were able to build themselves a meeting house. Quaker Ambrose Crowley leased the land for a nominal rent and a basic structure was erected which has been sympathetically added to over the years. The building is Grade II listed and is still being used for its original purpose as a Friends Meeting House.

8. John Wesley

Methodism has traditionally had strong roots in the Black Country, but this was not always so. The 20th of October 1743 saw the start of anti-Methodist riots which almost cost the life of John Wesley, one of the founders of the Methodist movement. He had come to preach from the 'horse block' at the High Bullen in Wednesbury. Later that same day he was forcibly taken by an angry mob from Wednesbury to see two magistrates but then fell into the hands of a more aggressive mob from Walsall. Wesley was in fear of his life and began to pray. The leader of the mob, George Clifton, was so moved that he spared Wesley, but the violence against Methodists continued into 1744.

9. Independent Order of Rechabites

In the 19th century friendly societies known locally as 'sick and draw clubs' were popular. Often run from public houses they were meant to help with things such as health care and death benefits but often just served to benefit the landlords and encourage drinking. The Independent Order of Rechabites was formed by a group of Methodists in 1835. They were also a friendly society but required members to sign the pledge and abstain from alcohol. Branches were known as tents to reflect the Old Testament Biblical origins of the movement.

10. Lady Wulfruna (also spelt Wulfrun)

Lady Wulfruna was an Anglo-Saxon Noblewoman who was granted lands by King Aethelred II at Heantun. Wulfrun's Heantun is thought to be where the name Wolverhampton is derived from. In 994 she endowed an existing monastery of St Mary to establish a collegiate church whose canons held extensive lands around the present-day Wolverhampton, Willenhall, Wednesfield and elsewhere in the Black Country. The dedication would later change to that of St Peter's Collegiate Church. Today's church is mainly medieval apart from the chancel which is a Victorian restoration. Lady Wulfruna's name is still very much evident around Wolverhampton.

Black Country at war

The Black Country has played its part in most of the major conflicts of the last few hundred years and even earlier with the Anglo-Saxons and the Danes. Dudley Castle has been a major stronghold since around 1070 following the Norman Conquest of 1066. The English Civil War impacted on this area as both the Royalists holding Dudley Castle and the Parliamentarian Committee at Stafford regarded it as their territory, especially for the purposes of taxation. The Black Country was rather surprisingly bombed, albeit by mistake, during the First World War. During the Second World War evacuees from London were taken in, despite the Black Country and Birmingham being major industrial areas.

1. Who rested his army in the grounds of Himley Hall on the way to the battle of Naseby?

2. Dudley Castle is guarded by two cannons which were trophies from which war?

3. Who disguised King Charles II as a servant and smuggled him to Bristol and safety?

4. John Berryman, from Dudley, was awarded the Victoria Cross for his bravery during which famous event in 1854?

5. What nickname did Quarry Bank acquire during World War Two?

6. What was the name of the purpose build factory in Dudley which produced munitions during the First World War?

7. Who suffered a major defeat in the year 910 at the Battle of Wednesfield, also known as the Battle of Tettenhall?

8. Due to a navigational error, the Black Country was bombed in 1916 by a Zeppelin commanded by the uncle of which famous singer and film star?

9. The battle of Tipton Green, although really a skirmish, took place between which opposing forces?

10. Sergeant Anthony Booth, buried in Brierley Hill, was awarded the Victoria Cross for saving fifty men during which war of 1879?

Question 2 – Dudley Castle and cannons

Answers – Section 10

1. King Charles I

Charles I and his army marched through the Midlands in the summer of 1645 during the English Civil War. Richard Symonds was accompanying the Royalist army and kept a detailed diary of events. His *Diary of the Marches of the Royal Army* records that on the 15th of May 1645 the army camped for one night at Himley Hall. In those days the hall itself was a moated manor house. Symond's diary also records that 'one soldjer [sic] was hanged for mutiny'. Justice was swift in those days! The Royalist army went on to defeat at the ill-fated Battle of Naseby on the 14th of June 1645.

2. The Crimean War

The twin cannons which guard the Dudley Castle Keep are a much later addition to the site. Most likely they were captured at the siege of Sevastopol which took place over 1854 and 1855. They were presented to the Earl of Dudley in recognition of his support for the war effort. In 1913 a group of local youths managed to fire the cannons towards the town. Needless to say, the guns were spiked after that incident to prevent any further illicit firing!

3. Jane Lane

Following defeat at the Battle of Worcester, Charles II escaped first to White Ladies Priory and then Boscobel House where he hid in the oak tree. From there he was taken to Mosely Old Hall not far from Wolverhampton. He then travelled to the home of Royalist Colonel John Lane near Walsall. John's sister, Jane Lane, had a pass to visit a pregnant friend in Abbots Leigh near Bristol. A plan was hatched to disguise Charles as a servant and smuggle him with Jane to Bristol. From there, Charles travelled on to eventually secure a safe passage to France.

4. The Charge of the Light Brigade

John Berryman was born in Dudley on the 18th of July 1825. He enlisted in the 17th Lancers and rose to the rank of sergeant before taking part in the Crimean War. During the Battle of Balaklava, confusion over which guns to attack led to the famous Charge of the Light Brigade. Berryman reached the Russian guns, but his horse was shot from under him. Although wounded himself, Berryman went to the aid of Captain Webb, whose leg was shattered. Despite orders to save themselves, he and two other men carried Captain Webb back to safety, but he later died of his wounds. For his bravery that day John Berryman was awarded the Victoria Cross.

5. Holy City

Quarry Bank near Brierley Hill is known as 'Quarry Bonk' in the local dialect. The nickname 'Holy City' came about because of a remarkable incident during World War Two. A German bomber on its way back from a raid on Liverpool dropped two 500 kg high explosive Luft Mines or Parachute Mines on the High Street. Amazingly neither exploded. One ended up suspended by its parachute from the roof of the Liberal Club. If they had exploded Quarry Bank would have been devastated with great loss of life. Because these were mines, a Royal Navy Bomb Disposal team had to be called in to safely diffuse them. After such a miraculous escape Quarry Bank became known as 'Holy City'.

6. National Projectile Factory

In 1915 during the First World War, Britain was facing a shortage of artillery shells described as a 'shell scandal'. In order to increase capacity, the Government ordered the construction of National Projectile Factories to address the problem. The factory in

Dudley was completed in 1916 and amongst other things produced shells for the standard British 18 pounder field-gun. It employed around 4,000 workers, most of whom were women. They were known as munitionettes and were proud to be doing 'their bit' for the war effort on the home front.

7. The Vikings

A major battle between the Anglo-Saxons and the Vikings took place in the year 910. Opinions vary as to exactly where this occurred, which is why it is known as both the Battle of Wednesfield (Wodensfield) and the Battle of Tettenhall. The actual battle may have been fought somewhere between the two places as they are only four miles apart. Mercians and West Saxons dealt a decisive blow against the Northumbrian Vikings. Following this battle, Vikings would never again pose a serious threat to Mercia, and England would soon unite under one monarch.

8. Marlene Dietrich

On the 31st of January 1916 during the First World War, nine German Zeppelins got lost during an air raid on Liverpool. Two of the airships were so off course they arrived over the Black Country. L21 appeared first and meted out death and destruction from Tipton to Walsall thinking the Black Country was Liverpool. The commander of Zeppelin L21 was Max Dietrich, uncle to the famous singer and film star Marlene Dietrich. The second Zeppelin, L19, arrived later causing yet more damage.

9. Royalists and Parliamentarians

The first siege of Dudley Castle in the English Civil War took place in 1644. The Earl of Denbigh commanded a Parliamentarian force against the Royalist stronghold. Hearing about the imminent arrival of a Royalist force under Lord Wilmot, Denbigh attempted to withdraw. He was caught unawares, and a brief battle ensued at Tipton Green. Both sides claimed a victory. The Parliamentarians had the upper hand but were unable to resume the siege. Lord Wilmot's only objective was to end the siege which he achieved.

10. Anglo-Zulu War

Anthony Clarke Booth (1846-1899) was born in Nottingham. After retiring from the army, he settled in Brierley Hill and is buried in St Michael's Churchyard. He won the Victoria Cross for bravery during the Zulu attack on the Intombi River on the 12th of March 1879. Sergeant Booth, as he was then, avoided a massacre by rallying a few men and covering the retreat of 'fifty soldiers and others for a distance of three miles'. Booth's coolness under fire that day ensured that all of the men survived. On the 26th of June 1880 he was presented with the Victoria Cross by Queen Victoria herself.

Notable people

Many notable people have had cause to come to the Black Country in addition to those born here. Charles Dickens knew the area and included it in *The Old Curiosity Shop* although some of the buildings are said to have been based on nearby Shifnal. When Queen Victoria was invited by the Council to unveil the statue of her late Prince Albert in Wolverhampton, nobody really thought she would come as she was still mourning his death in 1861. She did agree, and in 1866 Wolverhampton had just nine days to prepare for the visit!

1. When Queen Victoria came to Wolverhampton to unveil the statue of Prince Albert in 1866, the first triumphal arch she passed through near Low Level station was made of what?

2. John Dudley acquired Dudley Castle from John de Sutton in the mid-16th century but is mainly remembered for his ill-fated attempt to do what?

3. Who did Edward Sutton invite to Dudley Castle for a prestigious event in 1575?

4. Which poet transformed his family estate at the Leasowes in Halesowen into one of the country's earliest and most celebrated landscape gardens?

5. The first public statue of a woman in Britain not to be a Royal is in Walsall, but who is she?

6. An influential dictionary was produced in 1755 by which former scholar of King Edward VI Grammar School in Stourbridge?

7. The Prince of Wales (later King Edward VIII) and Wallis Simpson often visited the Black Country to stay where?

8. Which Halesowen born author based his Midland novels on the Black Country and Birmingham?

9. Although born in Kidderminster, who was the postal reformer who spent much of his earlier life in Wolverhampton?

10. John Johnson Shaw, who lived in West Bromwich, was renowned for recording what?

Question 5 – Statue in Walsall

Answers – Section 11

1. Coal

After Prince Albert's death in 1861 a statue was commissioned by public subscription. Nobody expected Queen Victoria to agree to unveil it in 1866 but she did, leaving just nine days to prepare for the Royal visit. A series of triumphal arches were erected for the Queen to pass through. The first of these at the entrance to the Great Western Railway Station drive was made of coal representing mining in the area. The Earl of Dudley supplied the massive blocks of coal needed for the arch and a pyramid which was built nearby.

2. Contrived to put Lady Jane Grey on the throne of England

In 1532 John Sutton inherited Dudley Castle but lost it through debt. Ownership passed to Sir John Dudley in 1537. He became Lord Protector to the young Edward VI until his death in 1553. John Dudley then contrived to put his daughter in law Lady Jane Grey on the throne of England. She became known as the 'nine days queen' after Mary Tudor mounted a successful challenge for the throne. John Dudley, his son Guildford Dudley, and his wife the unfortunate Lady Jane Grey, were all executed for treason by 'Bloody Mary'.

3. Queen Elizabeth I

Another son of the executed John Dudley was Robert Dudley the Earl of Leicester. After the death of Queen Mary I in 1558 Elizabeth I succeeded to the throne. Robert Dudley became a particular favourite of Elizabeth. Dudley Castle had reverted to the Sutton family and in 1575 one of the most prestigious events in its history took place. During one of her progresses around the country Queen Elizabeth I herself paid a visit.

4. William Shenstone

Poet William Shenstone was born at The Leasowes in Halesowen. His early education was at a Dame school in Halesowen. The Dame herself was to become immortalised in one of Shenstone's most famous poems *The School Mistress*. By 1745 Shenstone was back at The Leasowes and set about transforming the estate. He created pathways around lakes and streams together with grassy areas and woodland. William Shenstone had invented landscape gardening and is even credited with coining the phrase.

5. Sister Dora

Dorothy Wyndlow Pattison (1832 – 1878) joined an Anglican order and arrived in Walsall to work at the cottage hospital as Sister Dora. When Pelsall Colliery flooded in 1872 she worked tirelessly day and night to support the families waiting at the pithead. Local railwaymen were so moved they bought her a pony and trap, so she didn't have to walk to see patients. Another terrible accident was the blast furnace explosion at Birchills Ironworks in 1875. Three men were killed outright, and twelve others suffered the most terrible burns. Sister Dora nursed them herself to try and contain infection but even so only two survived. The statue of Sister Dora unveiled in 1886 is believed to be the first ever public statue to a woman in Britain not to be a royal.

6. Dr Samuel Johnson

Samuel Johnson (1709 – 1784) was born in Lichfield. Part of his education was in Stourbridge at the King Edward VI Grammar School, now a college, in Lower High Street. Johnson was a boarder and possibly taught younger pupils as well during his stay there. Samuel Johnson, later Dr Johnson, is best remembered for his famous *Dictionary of the English Language*. It was first published in 1755, took over eight years to produce and contained 40,000 words with definitions.

7. Himley Hall

In the 1920's, William Humble Eric Ward, later 3rd Earl of Dudley, set about turning Himley Hall into a grand house fit for royalty. No expense was spared on lavish rooms, private cinema, and indoor swimming pool with a water slide. Himley Hall was a regular retreat for Edward, Prince of Wales, and Mrs Simpson. After he was crowned Edward VIII, the King is said to have stayed at Himley just prior to his abdication from the British throne in December 1936.

8. Francis Brett Young

One of the few novelists to write about the Black Country, although it is argued that J. R. R. Tolkien based his mines and forges of Mordor here. Born 1884 in Halesowen, Francis Brett Young initially followed his father into the medical profession and served in East Africa during the First World War. This experience and ill health saw him concentrate on his writing. Francis Brett Young often paints a grim picture of the Black Country with loosely disguised place names. Dudley becomes Dulston, Halesowen is Halesby, Wednesbury is Wednesford and so on. His best-known novel is *My Brother Jonathon* which has been adapted for both film and television.

9. Roland Hill

Although born in Kidderminster, Roland Hill spent the early part of his life in Wolverhampton. His family had fallen on hard times and moved into Horsehills Farm which was basic but cheap to rent. He became close friends with Caroline Pearson, the daughter of local Liberal Party leader Joseph Pearson. They would later marry at St Peter's Church Wolverhampton in 1827. In 1840, Roland Hill's reform of the postal system saw the introduction of the Penny Post and the Penny Black which was the world's first adhesive postage stamp.

10. Earthquakes

John Johnson Shaw (1873 – 1948) was born in Lower Gornal but spent most of his life in West Bromwich. A meeting with retired Professor John Milne whilst on holiday on the Isle of Wight in 1896 would spark Shaw's interest in seismology and the recording of earthquakes. By 1913 Shaw had improved the magnification of John Milne's original design by up to 500 times to invent the Milne-Shaw Seismograph utilising optical and photographic recording. Milne-Shaw seismographs built at his home in West Bromwich would be the standard equipment for measuring earthquakes right up until the 1960s.

On the cut

With no navigable rivers, and long before the advent of the railways, transportation of raw materials and finished goods was a serious problem. It was solved with the coming of the canals. In a relatively short space of time the canal network grew up around the Black Country, Birmingham and beyond. The canals were not a rapid method of moving goods, but large quantities and heavy loads could be easily transported far in excess of any road transport at the time.

1. Who was engaged to 'cut' the first canal between Birmingham and the Black Country?

2. The impressive Galton Bridge in Smethwick was the work of which civil engineer?

3. What is unusual about the Delph 'Nine Locks' in Brierley Hill?

4. Opened in 1858 with double towpaths, which was the last major canal tunnel to be built in Britain?

5. What were the workers called who built the canals and later the railways?

6. In its heyday, how were narrowboats propelled through the Dudley Canal Tunnel?

7. An unpowered canal boat designed to be pulled behind a powered boat was known as a what?

8. Who pioneered the use of iron hulls in 1787 with the launch of the Trial in Shropshire following experiments in the Black Country?

9. What were the canal Roving Bridges designed to do?

10. What was the purpose of the canalside Bonded Warehouse at Stourbridge?

Question 10 – Stourbridge Bonded Warehouse

Answers – Section 12

1. James Brindley

In 1761 James Brindley was engaged to 'cut' a canal for the Duke of Bridgewater. The success of this was not lost on Birmingham industrialists such as Mathew Boulton. Birmingham as a developing manufacturing area lacked mineral resources. Brindley was employed to build a canal from Birmingham and through to the coalfields of the Black Country. The first shipment of coal reached Birmingham by canal in November 1769. By 1772 the final section to Aldersley was completed, with the new canal revolutionising the export of raw materials from the Black Country to Birmingham.

2. Thomas Telford

In 1824, Thomas Telford began improving Brindley's Old Main Line canal by constructing his New Main Line from Gas Street Basin to Tipton. Galton Bridge was built by Telford in 1829 to span the New Main Line at Smethwick over the impressive Galton Valley which had been dug out to take the new canal. It was constructed to carry a road, Roebuck Lane, and when opened Galton Bridge had the highest single span in the world at 151 feet (46 metres) wide.

3. There are only eight locks!

Although there are now only eight, Delph Locks on the Dudley No. 1 Canal in Brierley Hill is still known locally as the 'Nine Locks'. Originally built by Thomas Dadford in 1779 mining subsidence meant that a new straight flight of eight was constructed in the 1850s. The old top and bottom locks were retained but six new ones were built in between. Just to add to the general confusion, a pub near the bottom of the flight is called The Tenth Lock!

4. **Netherton Canal Tunnel**

Netherton Canal Tunnel was built to relieve congestion on the Dudley Canal Tunnel. The first sod of earth was turned by the Earl of Dudley in 1855 and the tunnel opened in 1858. The tunnel is 1.72 miles long and unusually it has towpaths on both sides and when opened was lit by gas. Later on, electric lights would replace the original gas lighting. Netherton Canal Tunnel marked the end of an era as it was the last to be opened in the Canal Age at a time when the railways were already taking precedence.

5. **Navvies**

The building of the canals and later the railways required thousands of manual labourers. The early canals used to be known as navigations. Those who built them were known as navigators and this was shortened to navvies. Nowadays, 'navvy' is a somewhat derogatory term, but these early canal builders were skilled at 'navigating' new waterways. With the demise of canal building the skills of the navvies to excavate vast tracts of land transferred readily to the building of the newer railways.

6. **By legging them through**

Dudley Canal Tunnel was opened to narrowboats in 1792. At 1¾ miles in length, it is the second longest navigable canal tunnel in England. However, this is disputed as it actually consists of the main tunnel, Lord Ward's tunnel and Castle Mill Basin. It was without a towpath so horses, the main motive power at the time, could not pull the narrowboats through. Originally, the only way to get narrowboats through was by 'legging' them. That is, bargees would lie on their backs and propel the boats through by walking along the tunnel walls.

7. **A butty**

On the canal network, a butty is an unpowered cargo boat which is towed by another powered boat. Once steam and diesel power replaced horses to draw narrowboats, butty boats became a familiar sight on the canals as they increased the load which could be carried. The term 'butty' is not restricted to the Black Country and may simply mean 'buddy'. In Black Country collieries a butty or chartermaster was a middleman who employed the miners directly, similar to the foggers in the nail and small chain trades.

8. John 'Iron Mad' Wilkinson

The iron hulled 'Trial' was built by John Wilkinson and launched onto the River Severn in July 1787. Trial was an unpowered barge and often considered to be the first iron vessel of its type. This was not actually the case, but Trial was certainly a pioneering attempt to find an alternative to wood. Experiments had initially been carried out at Wilkinson's Bradley Iron Works in Bilston. Although launched on the River Severn, the intention was most likely to use Trial on the nearby Birmingham Canal as was the case with later iron hulled barges.

9. To enable horses pulling narrowboats to swap towpaths without unhitching the towline

Roving bridges were a very clever solution to a common problem in the days of horse drawn narrowboats. Often the towpath would swap sides meaning the horse would have to be unhitched, taken over a bridge and hitched up again. Roving bridges solved this problem by allowing the horse to cross without the towline getting caught up on the bridge. Designs varied, but one method was to have the ramps on the same side of the bridge and turn the horse through 360 degrees. This would mean the towline could pass through the bridge unhindered.

10. To store taxable goods

The Bonded Warehouse was a building where taxable goods such as alcohol and tobacco could be securely stored. The Bonded Warehouse in Stourbridge was built in 1779 and used to store such taxable goods until the importer paid the required duty or tax. The building was also used to store non-taxable goods awaiting shipment. Stourbridge Bonded Warehouse has been preserved and is now used for a variety of functions and events.

Road and rail

Even with an extensive canal network roads were still important and decent roads meant faster travel. The better quality roads required a toll to be paid to use them hence the number of toll houses which can still be seen. It was really the coming of the railways which led to the decline and eventual demise of the toll roads when local councils took them over in the 1870s. Large factories and mines could have their own branch lines which would mean quick and easy connection to the entire mainline railway network.

1. A train ride on the shortest branch line in Britain can be taken where?

2. The Oxford, Worcester & Wolverhampton railway used to be known by what acronym?

3. Toll houses used to be a familiar sight on canals, bridges, and what type of roads?

4. The Wolverhampton Everlasting was an example of what?

5. In 1902, why did Wolverhampton adopt an unusual system of electrified studs in the road?

6. What was the name of the first steam locomotive to run in America which was built by Foster and Rastrick of Stourbridge?

7. Foster and Rastrick also built the famous Agenoria which ran on the Kingswinford (Shutt End) Railway from 1829 but where can she now be found?

8. What was the Shutt End Railway originally constructed to transport?

9. John Rastrick was one of the three judges at what in 1829?

10. What replaced Wolverhampton's trams to form one of the most extensive networks of its type in Britain?

Question 3 – Toll house in Smethwick High Street

Answers – Section 13

1. Stourbridge Town to Stourbridge Junction

The branch line from Stourbridge Town to Stourbridge Junction was earmarked for closure under the Beeching cuts but had a reprieve in 1965. The line used to be longer when freight was carried to and from Stourbridge Canal Basin over a bridge in Foster Street. Following closure of the goods branch, the bridge was demolished in 1967. Stourbridge Town Branch Line is just 0.8 miles or 1287 metres long making it the shortest branch line in Britain and possibly Europe. Nowadays, two Class 139 Parry People Movers transport passengers along the line.

2. The Old Worse and Worse

Of course, when the line passed through the Black Country it was known as the 'Old Wuss and Wuss' in the dialect, being an acronym of the Oxford, Worcester and Wolverhampton Railway. When the OW&WR was authorised by Parliament in 1845, it was to be 89 miles of dual gauge track being both Stephenson's 4ft 8½ inch narrow gauge and Brunel's 7ft ¼ inch broad gauge. Stephenson's narrow gauge would eventually become the 'standard' gauge. Locally, the Stourbridge to Dudley section of the line opened to passengers in 1852. It did not properly serve Wolverhampton for goods and passengers until 1854 due to legal issues with the GWR.

3. Turnpike roads

These were administered by local Turnpike Trusts once permission had been granted by Parliament. Toll houses and gates would be set up and a sliding scale of charges was levied depending on what was being transported. By law, all of the money collected had to be ploughed back into the roads to pay staff such as the toll house keepers and to cover the cost of repairs. The name 'turnpike' may originate from the use of a hinged pole, a bit like a pikestaff, instead of a gate and turned to give access.

4. **A horse drawn stagecoach**

    In the days before the railways long distance travel for most folk meant the many horse drawn stagecoaches which crisscrossed the country. Coaching inns provided refreshment, a change of horses and a bed on long journeys. Stagecoaches often had inventive names. The Worcester Journal in 1822 regularly advertised the Wolverhampton Everlasting as leaving the Unicorn Inn every afternoon at three. This coach called at Stourbridge, Dudley, and Sedgley in the Black Country before arriving at the Star and Garter in Wolverhampton. The return journey would be every morning except Sunday.

5. **To power electric trams**

    In 1902, Wolverhampton converted its existing horse drawn tram system to electrification. To avoid overhead wires an unusual system using Lorain Studs connected to a buried power cable in the road was employed. The trams had metal skids to pick up the supply. The system worked but was not compatible with any other of the Black Country networks. By 1921 Wolverhampton was converting its tram lines to the more conventional overhead wires.

6. **The Stourbridge Lion**

    One of four locomotives built by Foster and Rastrick of Stourbridge, she was shipped to America in crates for final assembly there. Someone painting the boiler front noticed dents that looked like a Lion's head. From then on, she was called the Stourbridge Lion. The locomotive is recognised as being the first to run on a commercial railroad in America although the tracks proved to be unsuitable for such a heavy engine. The remains of the Stourbridge Lion are owned by the Smithsonian Institution.

7. The National Railway Museum in York

Agenoria was a sister engine to the Stourbridge Lion built by Foster and Rastrick and the only one of the four not to be exported to America. The engine was named after the relatively minor Roman Goddess of activity and industry. Agenoria was built to run on Lord Dudley's new Shutt End railway and was the first standard gauge (4 ft 8½ in) locomotive to run in the Midlands. Vast crowds attended the opening of the Shutt End railway on the 2nd of June 1829.

8. Coal

James Foster of the Stourbridge based company Foster and Rastrick signed an agreement in 1827 to build a railway for Lord Dudley (4th Viscount Dudley and Ward). This was to enable coal from the Corbyns Hall Colliery at Shutt End to be transported to the Staffordshire & Worcestershire (Staffs & Worcs) Canal at Ashwood Basin, Kingswinford. The railway ran between two inclined planes where the weight of full coal waggons was used to draw empty waggons back up. When the railway officially opened on the 2nd of June 1829 hundreds of people enjoyed train rides in the open wagons.

9. The Rainhill Trials

John Urpeth Rastrick, of the Stourbridge based Foster, Rastrick and Company, was one of the leading railway engineers of his day. He had assisted Richard Trevithick in developing his puffing Billy locomotive and engineered both the Agenoria and Stourbridge Lion. In 1829 he was invited to be one of just three judges at the famous Rainhill Trials locomotive competition. It was here that one locomotive clearly won the day, and that was the innovative Stephenson's Rocket.

10. Trolley buses

Wolverhampton only installed overhead wires for its trams in 1921, but by 1928 these had been replaced by trolley buses which used the overhead wires for electrical power but didn't need the tracks. Companies such as Wolverhampton based Sunbeam and Guy were supplying trolley buses all around the Black Country and beyond. Trolley buses were very popular and environmentally friendly being electrically powered. Despite this, the very last of Wolverhampton's trolley bus fleet ceased operating on the route to Dudley in March 1967 to be replaced by motor buses.

Powered vehicles

Bicycle manufacturing was already well established, particularly in Wolverhampton, and the development of small, relatively efficient internal combustion engines towards the end of the 19th century encouraged the development of motorcycles. Cars and vans soon followed, and in its heyday, there were over fifty vehicle manufacturers in the Black Country alone. Only one sports car manufacturer established in the 1980s still remains.

1. John Marston founded which Wolverhampton company producing cycles, motorcycles, and cars including world speed record breakers?

2. AJS is a well-known name for motorcycles but what do the initials stand for?

3. Villiers in Wolverhampton started out producing bicycle pedals for John Marston, then an effective cycle freewheel, and later on small petrol engines, but where did they get their unusual name from?

4. Which Black Country manufacturer made Malcolm Campbell's first Blue Bird land speed record breaking car?

5. What was the rather frolicsome name given to the small Villier's powered three-wheeler car pictured?

6. Which Wolverhampton company specialized in commercial vehicles, trolley buses, motor buses and coaches?

7. Who was the first driver to break the 200 miles per hour land speed barrier in 1927 driving a Sunbeam car?

8. Which Tipton based vehicle manufacturer built the Thunderbolt land speed record breaking car?

9. The last of a long line of Black Country car manufacturers, which company established in 1983 to produce small sports cars is now developing driverless vehicles?

10. Which luxury sports car manufacturer was based in West Bromwich until it closed in 1976?

Question 5 – Villiers powered three-wheeler car

Answers – Section 14

1. Sunbeam

John Marston owned a japanning works in Wolverhampton and decided to expand into the production of bicycles. In 1888 he registered the name Sunbeam for his new enterprise. Credit for the name goes to John's wife Ellen who saw a shaft of sunlight reflecting off a gleaming new bicycle frame and said it looked just like a sunbeam. In fact, the factory was known as Sunbeamland. The company would go on to become one of the most illustrious names in the production of bicycles, motorcycles, and cars.

2. Albert John (Jack) Stevens

Engineering blacksmith Joe Stevens from Wednesfield had five sons. Four of these, John, George, Harry, and Joseph formed the Stevens Motor Manufacturing Company to produce petrol engines including engines for motorcycles. In 1909 they founded another company in Retreat Street Wolverhampton but didn't want to use the same name, so they chose to use initials only. The only brother to have three initials was Albert John Stevens known as Jack. His initials were used and the famous AJS name was born.

3. Villiers Street

John Marston of Sunbeam was producing top quality bicycles but was dissatisfied with the bought in pedals. Son Charles had machinery imported from America to manufacture their own high-quality pedals. Another factory was needed and so John purchased a small japanning works in Villiers Street Wolverhampton and the new company took the Villiers name. The street is named after Charles Pelham Villiers, the longest ever continuously serving member of Parliament. He represented Wolverhampton and then Wolverhampton South for 63 years and 6 days.

4. **Sunbeam**

The world land speed record in 1922 was broken by a 350 horsepower Sunbeam. The car reached a speed of 133.75 miles per hour and was driven by Kenelm Lee Guinness, a member of the famous brewing family. He also designed a much-improved spark plug and marketed it using his own initials – KLG. Malcolm Campbell bought the car and named it Blue Bird after the play by Maurice Maeterlinck. He set two land speed records driving the Sunbeam including 150.76 miles per hour at Pendine Sands in 1925. Malcolm Campbell continued to use the name for his record breakers, but his son Donald, also a famous record breaker, would later change it to one word, Bluebird.

5. **Frisky**

Villiers became well known for small petrol engines such as those used in motorcycles and even small cars. In 1913 they developed a highly successful 269 cc two stroke engine. They continued to develop small engines and in 1956 presented their two millionth engine, a 225 cc single cylinder two stroke, to the London Science Museum. In 1957 the little Frisky appeared, built by Henry Meadows (Vehicles Ltd) of Wolverhampton. Powered by a Villiers 250 cc petrol engine the Frisky was available in different variants including the three-wheeler which could be driven on a motorcycle licence. Although the little cars were well received, they did not sell well and in 1959 another small car from Longbridge took the world by storm. The Mini had arrived.

6. **Guy Motors**

In May 1914 Sidney Guy left his job as Works Manager for Sunbeam and set up Guy Motors to manufacture commercial vehicles. He built his factory in the Fallings Park area of Wolverhampton and to start with manufactured a 30-cwt lorry. Over the years, the name Guy would be seen on lorries, charabancs, coaches, trolleybuses, motor buses and military vehicles including armoured cars. By the 1970s an earlier disastrous venture in South Africa, and a merger encouraged by the Labour Government which created British Leyland, ultimately sounded the death knell for Guy Motors.

7. Henry Segrave

In the 1920s, the great land speed record to break was 200 miles per hour. The man to do it was Henry Segrave who was knighted in 1929 in recognition of his achievements. The record-breaking 1,000 hp (according to the publicity at least) car was built by Sunbeam specifically to break the elusive barrier and was powered by two 22.5 litre aero engines. The record was finally broken on the 29th of March 1927 at Daytona Beach when Segrave achieved a speed of 203.79 mph.

8. Beans Industries

After the First World War, A. Harper, Sons & Bean began producing motor cars. The chassis would be made at Tipton and driven to Dudley to be fitted with bodies. The cars were simply known as the Bean. Following a takeover by Hadfields, the company became Bean Cars Limited in 1926. In 1933 Hadleys relaunched the company as Beans Industries. In 1937, the last car to be built at Tipton was George Eyston's record breaking Thunderbolt. It took just six weeks to build and in 1938 at Bonneville Salt Flats Eyston set the World Land Speed Record at 357.5 miles per hour. The event is commemorated in Tipton with Thunderbolt Way and Bonneville Close.

9. Westfield Sports Cars Limited

In its heyday there were over fifty powered vehicle manufacturers in the Black Country area. At the time of writing there is just one established car maker and that is Westfield of Kingswinford. Founded in 1983, Westfield produce road and track sports cars in both fully assembled and kit form. The company is carrying on a long tradition of sports car manufacture in the Black Country and also looking to the future with their autonomous POD driverless vehicles.

10. Jensen

The Jensen Brothers, Alan and Richard, started Jensen Motors Limited after taking control of W. J. Smith and Sons of Carters Green West Bromwich in 1934. Initially they were specialist luxury car body makers but would go on to manufacture complete vehicles. Jensen also made lorries and even a luxury coach, although very few of these were produced. The name most associated with Jensen is the Interceptor. The name first appeared on cars built between 1950 and 1957. In 1966 a new Italian designed hand-built luxury Interceptor was launched which was very well received and stayed in production until 1976 when mounting losses forced Jensen to close its doors.

Connections with the sea

The Black Country is as far from the sea in any direction as it is possible to get. Nevertheless, there are a surprising number of connections with the sea. Famously, Noah Hingley and Sons are known for making the anchors and chains for the Titanic and her sister ships but the very first iron steamship to put to sea was also fabricated here.

1.   Why did sailors have reason to be thankful to Chance Brothers of Smethwick?

2.   James Eaton is buried in West Bromwich and during the Battle of Trafalgar served as a midshipman on which warship later to be immortalized in a painting by Turner?

3.   Which Stourbridge glass company supplied the White Star Line with high-class crystalware for the ill-fated ocean liner RMS Titanic?

4.   In addition to the Titanic, which other two Olympic class liners had their anchors and chains made in the Black Country?

5.   Built at the Horseley (also spelt Horsley) Ironworks of Tipton, what was the name of the first iron steamship to put to sea in 1822?

6. Being so far from the sea, how was the first iron steamship transported from Tipton to London?

7. What part did John Wesley Woodward from West Bromwich play in the sinking of the Titanic?

8. As well as the Titanic, Noah Hingley and Sons made the anchors and chains for which other ill-fated vessel which sank off the coast of Ireland in 1915?

9. Samuel Taylor and Sons of Brierley Hill supplied the chains and anchors for which Cunard 'Queens' of the sea?

10. A replica of the huge Titanic centre anchor was made for the Channel 4 series Titanic: The Mission in 2010 but where can the anchor now be found?

Question 5 – The world's first iron steamship

Answers – Section 15

1. Lighthouses

Chance Brothers of Smethwick supplied the glass for the Crystal Palace in London which housed the Great Exhibition of 1851. At the exhibition they showcased a radical new design for lighthouse lenses inspired by James Timmins Chance. This was to prove so successful that Chance built a new lighthouse works in order to satisfy the worldwide demand. They not only produced the optics but also the machinery to rotate the lenses and other components to equip lighthouses.

2. The Fighting Temeraire

James Eaton retired to West Bromwich after a distinguished career in the Royal Navy and is buried at All Saints Church. During the Battle of Trafalgar on the 21st of October 1805, James Eaton was a signal midshipman on HMS Temeraire. He had the honour of being the first to repeat Nelson's famous flag signal from HMS Victory, 'England expects that every man will do his duty'. Turner painted his now famous picture of the Temeraire as the venerable old warship was being towed up the Thames to Rotherhithe to be dismantled in 1838 and exhibited *The Fighting Temeraire* in 1839.

3. Stuart Crystal

Stuart and Sons of Stourbridge were the producers of the world famous Stuart Crystal. Glassmaking and decorating had developed from the seventeenth century when the once familiar glass cones began to appear. Stourbridge glass was a byword for quality and could be found gracing the tables of the wealthy around the world. When the White Star Line needed the finest quality glassware for the Titanic, they turned to Stuart and Sons to supply it.

4. RMS Olympic and RMS Britannic

The story of what happened to the Titanic on her maiden voyage in 1912 is well known but she was one of three similar Olympic Class liners ordered by the White Star Line. Noah Hingley and Sons of Netherton had the contracts to supply anchors and chains from Harland and Wolff for all three. Olympic survived the longest, setting sail on her maiden voyage in 1911 and making her last voyage in 1935 after which she was sold for scrap. At the outbreak of the First World War, Britannic was converted into a hospital ship but sank following an explosion in 1916 after reportedly striking a mine. Unlike the Titanic, nearly everybody escaped in the lifeboats.

5. The Aaron Manby

The Horseley (also spelt Horsley) Ironworks of Tipton cast the ironwork for the Galton Bridge in Smethwick and many others but is also renowned for having constructed the world's first iron steamship to go to sea, the Aaron Manby. Initial steam trials took place on the River Thames between the London and Battersea bridges. Following successful trials history was made in June 1822 when the Aaron Manby crossed the English Channel to reach Paris under the command of Captain Charles Napier.

6. By canal!

It was Captain Charles Napier, Royal Navy, who had the original idea of building an iron steamship. He collaborated with Aaron Manby, who was a partner in Horseley Iron Works, and who gave the ship its name. It was constructed of prefabricated sections which meant it could be transported by canal. An initial 'loose' assembly took place in Tipton to ensure everything fitted together as it should. It did, and the vessel was dismantled and loaded onto canal boats ready for final assembly at the Surrey Canal Dock in Rotherhithe, London.

7. He played in the band as the Titanic went down

John Wesley Woodward was born in West Bromwich on the 11th of September 1879. By the early 1900s he was living in Oxford and making himself known as a professional cellist. After a spell in Eastbourne John joined the White Star Line as a musician and spent some time on the Olympic before joining the Titanic. As the ship went down, he was one of the brave musicians who played on to try and calm the passengers. None of the musicians survived.

8. The Lusitania

Considering the Black Country is about as far from the sea as it is possible to get in any direction, the area supplied chains and anchors for some of the world's most famous ships. One of these was the ill-fated RMS Lusitania whose anchors and chains were supplied by Noah Hingley and Sons. On a return voyage from America, the Lusitania was torpedoed by a German U-boat on the 7th of May 1915 off the coast of Ireland. Nearly 1,200 passengers and crew died.

9. The Queen Mary and the Queen Elizabeth

Noah Hingley and Sons were not the only Black Country company supplying anchors and chains for the world's greatest ocean-going liners. Samuel Taylor and Sons of Brettell Lane, Brierley Hill were contracted by Cunard to supply the anchors and chains for two of the most famous luxury liners, the Queen Mary, and the Queen Elizabeth. Taylors also supplied equipment for the Royal Yacht Brittania. The two Queens were withdrawn from service in the 1960s and HMY Britannia in 1997.

10. Netherton

The full-size replica of the Titanic anchor, made for Channel 4's Titanic: The Mission in 2010 was intended to be brought to Netherton hauled by twenty heavy horses and following the reverse route of the original. In the event, for the safety of the horses, the final leg of the journey was completed by tractor. The anchor was exhibited outside the Black Country Living Museum whilst a permanent base was created. It is now on permanent display on the site of the old marketplace in Netherton not far from where the original anchor began its fateful journey in 1911 to Belfast and the RMS Titanic.

Pubs and breweries

One thing the Black Country can certainly take pride in is the quality of the real ales brewed here, and the traditional pubs that serve them. This long tradition was almost lost when the big breweries were pushing their keg beers. The Campaign for Real Ale (CAMRA) was formed in 1971 and could find only four traditional home-brew pubs left in the country. One of these was here in the Black Country. The situation has now come full circle and the discerning beer drinker is now literally spoilt for choice!

1.   Known locally as the 'Siden House' and originally named the Glynne Arms what is this famous Black Country pub now called?

2.   What is the proper name for Batham's Bull and Bladder pub and brewery in Brierley Hill?

3.   The 1830 Beer Act allowed many Black Country folk to purchase a beerhouse licence for two guineas in order to brew and sell their own beer, but whose Tory government introduced it?

4.   Which major brewery in Dudley was named after a mother and her sons?

5.   What is the quote from Shakespeare's *Two Gentleman of Verona* on the frontage of the Bull and Bladder pub in Brierley Hill?

6. What is the proper name of the Black Country pub identified by CAMRA in the 1970s as one of only four remaining home-brew houses in the country?

7. Cape Hill in Smethwick was the home to which major brewery?

8. Which lady brewer gives her name to the Victorian tower brewery based at the Beacon Hotel in Sedgley?

9. Woodsetton's Park Inn has been the site of which brewery since 1915?

10. The oldest pub in Wednesbury, where infamous highwayman Dick Turpin allegedly stayed, is called what?

Question 8 – The Beacon Hotel Sedgley

Answers – Section 16

1. The Crooked House at Himley

Possibly the best-known pub in the Black Country and one of the most unusual. Originally a farmhouse, it was once owned by Sir Stephen Richard Glynne which is where the name 'Glynne Arms' came from. His sister was married to the Liberal Prime Minister William Gladstone. Mining subsidence from the Glynne Estate has caused part of the building to sink by several feet. The whole interior confuses the senses. Marbles appear to roll uphill, and a clock looks ready to fall over but is perfectly upright! For many years the pub was known locally as the 'Siden House' or the 'Crooked House'. Siden in Black Country dialect means not upright or crooked. Since 2002 the pub has been officially known as the Crooked House.

2. The Vine Inn

At the time of writing Bathams has twelve pubs in and around the Black Country. Officially called the Vine Inn, the pub at the Delph in Brierley Hill is much better known as the Bull and Bladder. It is also the home of the Bathams Brewery. Its history goes back to 1882 when Daniel Batham started brewing at the White Horse in Cradley Heath.

3. The Duke of Wellington

Arthur Wellesley, 1st Duke of Wellington, is mainly remembered for the Battle of Waterloo but he was also a politician and Prime Minister. Wellington's Tory Government introduced the Beer Act of 1830 which revolutionised the way beer was sold and more importantly, who could sell it. On payment of two guineas to the local excise collectors virtually anyone could open a beerhouse for the sale of beer and cider only. Many beerhouses were small and might consist of just one room given over to the sale and consumption of mainly home brewed beer. Many older Black Country pubs started life as beerhouses.

4. Julia Hanson and Sons Limited

The brewery was started by Julia Hanson after first founding a wines and spirits business in 1847. Julia started brewing a mild beer which proved popular and by the time she died in 1894 her sons Thomas and William were involved in the business. They acquired the Peacock Brewery in Upper High Street Dudley, and after having had a new brewery built registered the company as Julia Hanson and Sons Limited in 1902. Hansons was acquired by Wolverhampton and Dudley Breweries Limited in 1943 and continued to brew until it closed in 1992.

5. "Blessing of your heart you brew good ale"

The quote comes from Shakespeare's *The Two Gentlemen of Verona* Act 3 Scene 1. As such, it is entirely appropriate to be adorning the front of a real ale pub and brewery. Less obvious is the Bull and Bladder name which the pub is universally known by. It seemed fairly common in the Black Country for butchers to purchase a two guinea beerhouse licence and turn a room over to selling beer. This was the case with the Vine Inn and why it is still known as the Bull and Bladder.

6. The Old Swan Inn

Better known as Ma Pardoes, the Old Swan Inn is on the Halesowen Road in the centre of Netherton. In the early 1970s the Campaign for Real Ale (CAMRA) identified it as being one of only four remaining home-brew pubs in the whole country. At that time, traditional real ale had almost died out in favour of the keg beer offerings from the big breweries. Doris (Ma) Pardoe was the licensee after her husband Fred died and managed the pub and brewery up until her own death in 1984. The pub continues to maintain the tradition of brewing real ales on the premises.

7.   Mitchells and Butlers

Although sometimes associated with Birmingham, the Mitchells and Butlers Cape Hill Brewery was in Smethwick which has never been part of Birmingham. Mitchells and Butlers was formed in 1898 when Henry Mitchell & Company Limited of Cape Hill merged with Butler's Crown Brewery Limited of Broad Street Birmingham. All production was switched to the Cape Hill Brewery which was greatly enlarged. The brewery closed in 2002 and by 2005 was being demolished. Little remains apart from the M&B War Memorial which remains in situ on Barrett Street.

8.   Sarah Hughes

Sarah Hughes took over the Beacon Hotel on Bilston Street, Sedgley in 1921. She began brewing a traditional strong dark beer, Dark Ruby Mild, which is still brewed today. The Grade II listed Victorian pub retains many of its original features including the tower brewery which is still in use. As well as the Dark Ruby Mild, a range of beers are brewed which are frequent award winners at beer festivals around the country.

9.   Holden's Brewery

In 1898 Alfred Holden and his new wife Lucy took on the tenancy of The Britannia Inn, Netherton. By 1910 they had moved to the Summer House in Woodsetton and acquired the nearby Park Inn in 1915 which is where they moved to in 1920. The brewing side of the business expanded with a bottling plant added later in the 1940s and an increasing estate of pubs. At the time of writing Holdens has nineteen real ale pubs. Brewery tours are run regularly and the brewery also has its own shop.

10. Ye Olde Leathern Bottel

The origins of this ancient pub in Vicarage Road, Wednesbury are unknown, but it is believed to have originally been a row of cottages and a coach house before becoming a pub. The 1510 date painted on the outside may or may not be accurate, but the building is certainly old and deserving of its reputation as the oldest pub in Wednesbury. Legend has it that notorious highwayman Dick Turpin even stayed here – but then many old black and white pubs in the Midlands claim that dubious honour!

All creatures great and small

In 2020 the Black Country was awarded UNESCO Global Geopark status, reflecting both the industrial heritage of the area and its remarkable geology, including the fossil bearing limestone found at Wrens Nest, near Dudley. These fossils contain the remains of creatures which were alive millions of years ago when the Black Country was covered by a great sea. Nearer the present day, Black Country pastimes for working folk included such things as pigeon and whippet racing. It was common for drinking establishments to be described as 'pigeon pubs' or 'dog pubs' depending on the principal interests of the regulars.

1. Bear baiting, cock-fighting, dog-fighting and other barbarous 'sports' were banned, although not altogether successfully, by the Cruelty to Animals Act in which year?

    a. 1835

    b. 1845

    c. 1855

    d. 1865

2. What is Calymene blumenbachii better known as in the Black Country?

3. Where did the last pit ponies in the Black Country work?

4. The Throstles is an old nickname for which football club?

5. In the Black Country what is a Bobowler?

6. What popular local breed of dog was recognized in the 1930s by the Kennel Club?

7. What is the well-known saying attributed to Gornal folk?

8. Dudley Zoological Gardens opened in May 1937 but who's original idea was it?

9. As well as racing or homing pigeons, what other type of pigeon was popular with fanciers in the Black Country and Birmingham?

10. The nickname of Walsall Football Club is The Saddlers but since 1888 the club symbol has been what?

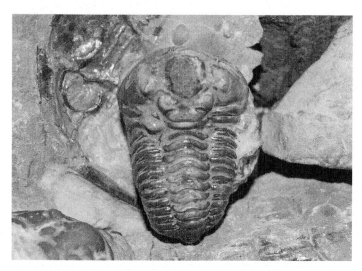

Question 2 - Calymene blumenbachii

Answers – Section 17

1. **a. 1835**

    South Durham MP Joseph Pease introduced the Bill which led to the Cruelty to Animals Act of 1835. He was a member of The Society for the Prevention of Cruelty to Animals (SCA) which became the RSPCA in 1840 when Queen Victoria permitted use of the royal 'R'. The Act was successful in banning bear baiting and bull baiting but less so with dog fighting and cock fighting which went 'underground' and carried on in the Black Country as elsewhere. Bull baiting as a 'sport' had its origins in the medieval belief that it tenderised the meat at market before slaughter.

2. **The Dudley Bug**

    The abundance of limestone in the Black Country in areas such as Wrens Nest makes this one of the world's most important sites for fossils. They would be found by quarrymen digging out the limestone and one of the most common was the Trilobite Calymene blumenbachii. This was nicknamed the 'Dudley Bug', sometimes called the 'Dudley Locust', and appears on the Dudley County Borough coat of arms which was officially granted in 1957.

3. **Baggeridge Colliery**

    Baggeridge was the last deep coal mine in the Black Country and pit ponies were living and working underground right up until its closure in 1968. Baggeridge was a large pit and in its heyday had stables for over 100 ponies. There were strict regulations regarding how long pit ponies could work for and at Baggeridge the stalls were warm, airy, and lit by electric lights. Although they worked hard, a bond would build up between the ponies and their handlers. When the remaining eight ponies came to the surface for the last time, they all had good local homes waiting for them.

The head horse keeper, Harold Worton, took two ponies himself to look after.

4.   West Bromwich Albion

Throstle is an old word for a Thrush or Song Thrush and was commonly used in the Black Country. After West Bromwich Albion was formed in 1878, they played at a succession of grounds until settling at The Hawthorns in 1900. The area took its name from Hawthorn bushes which used to grow there. These would attract Song Thrushes hence the nickname of the Throstles. Another theory is that before moving to The Hawthorns the team used a hotel as a base. The landlady kept a Song Thrush in a cage and the club secretary suggested they use it as a logo. Apparently, if it sang on a match day it was good omen!

5.   A large moth

Bobowler is an English Midlands word and not just restricted to the Black Country. Although author J. R. R. Tolkien spent his childhood in Birmingham, he also knew the Black Country and likely based his mines and forges of Mordor here. In his fictional language of Sindarin Mordor means Black Land. In his novella *Roverandom* he refers to bobowlers in chapter three but uses the alternative spelling of bob-owlers.

6.   Staffordshire Bull Terrier

James Hinks of Birmingham is generally credited with founding the Bull Terrier breed by crossing a Bulldog with a Black and Tan Terrier in the 19th century. Bull Terriers were originally bred as fighting dogs although dog fighting had been banned in 1835. The breed was particularly popular in the Black Country where they were known a miners' fighting dogs. It was mainly through the efforts of Joe Mallen and the Cradley Heath Club that

Staffordshire Bull Terriers were recognised as a distinct breed by the Kennel Club in the 1930s.

7. **'They put the pig on the wall to see the band go by'**

The origins of this saying are unclear, and it crops up in different parts of the country. In Dawley, Shropshire, the pig was supposedly put on the wall to watch Captain Webb's procession go by. He was the first person to swim the English Channel in 1875 and lived in Dawley. A postcard was issued with a pig looking over a wall and this was copied in Gornal but without Captain Webb. Another version has it that the Primitive Methodist band was going by and the diminutive drummer at the back carried straight on when he should have turned left because he couldn't see over the drum. A local wag quickly got his pig and propped his forelegs up against the wall to see the one-man band go by!

8. **The Third Earl of Dudley**

The Dudley Castle site was owned by the Earl of Dudley, and he formed a partnership with Earnest Marsh (of Marsh & Baxters) and Captain Frank Cooper who was looking to sell his stock of animals from Oxford Zoo. Dudley Zoo opened in May 1937 and on the first day proved so popular people had to be turned away after 50,000 visitors had been admitted.

9. **Tumblers or Rollers**

In the Black Country pastimes such as pigeon fancying offered a welcome relief from the hard graft of industry and mining. Many kept racing or homing pigeons but tumblers or rollers were also popular. These were performing birds who would be flown in a flock or 'kit' and judged on how well they would twist or somersault in unison with each other. Rapidly somersaulting or spinning pigeons were bred particularly in Birmingham and became known as Birmingham Rollers.

10. A Swift

The nickname of Walsall Football Club is the Saddlers due to the connection with leatherworking in the area. The emblem though is a Swift. The club started in 1888 when Walsall Town and Walsall Swifts merged to become Walsall Town Swifts. By 1895, the name Town Swifts had been dropped but the Swift as an emblem remained. Nowadays the Swift in the emblem points upwards whereas it used to point down.

Historic homes

The Black Country during the industrial revolution tends to be associated with substandard, overcrowded housing with little in the way of proper sanitation or even a clean water supply. It was not the case for everyone though. For those who could afford it, particularly industrialists and the aristocracy, the Black Country had some particularly fine historic homes.

1. Who was employed to landscape the grounds of Himley Hall in the 18th century?

2. What was the pictured building preserved on the Junction 1 M5 Motorway and A41 island at West Bromwich?

3. The Arts and Crafts interior at Wolverhampton's Wightwick Manor is one of the best surviving examples of furnishings by whose famous firm?

4. In an attempt to make Dudley Castle more comfortable, John Dudley had what constructed in the 16th century?

5. What was the name of the house near Walsall where the Lane family famously aided the escape of Charles II?

6. Which Grade 1 listed medieval building had been converted to tenements and lay hidden behind a modern façade until rescued by West Bromwich Corporation in the 1950s?

7. Who was invited to preach by William Whyley in the courtyard of the Oak House, West Bromwich, in 1774?

8. Which house in Kingswinford is directly connected with the Gunpowder Plot of 1605?

9. A number of follies including the Wychbury Hill Obelisk are associated with which Hagley family?

10. In the 1930s, Sir Geoffrey and Lady Rosalie Mander of Wightwick Manor began a unique collection of art based on which artistic movement?

Question 2 – (Copyright Richard Law)

Answers – Section 18

1. Lancelot 'Capability' Brown

Himley Hall was originally a moated manor house owned by the Lords of Dudley. The Ward family acquired the estate in 1628 through the marriage of Humble Ward to Frances Sutton, heiress to the estate. In 1740 the 6th Baron, John Ward, had the manor house replaced with a Palladian style mansion. The village of Himley was moved to accommodate parkland and a new church built in 1764. It was John's son, also John, who employed Lancelot 'Capability' Brown to landscape the parkland and create the Great Lake fed by a series of waterfalls and pools.

2. Gateway to Sandwell Hall

The building is called Arch Lodge and was once the gateway to the now demolished Sandwell Hall. The aristocratic Legge family, Earls of Dartmouth, had purchased the estate in 1701 and had Sandwell Hall built. By the mid-19th century Sandwell Hall was being affected by all the industry around it and in 1853 the family relocated to Patshull Hall which they had purchased in 1848. Sandwell Hall was demolished in 1928 and the estate is now Sandwell Valley Country Park. Arch Lodge is virtually all that remains of the once stately home.

3. William Morris

Wightwick Manor near Wolverhampton is a perfect example of a house designed and furnished in Arts and Crafts style. Morris, Marshall, Faulkener & Company supplied furniture, fittings, and wallpaper for the interior. Poems and quotations adorn the interior. In the drawing room the spirit of William Morris himself is evoked with a verse from the prologue to his poem *Earthly Paradise* in a painted glass window by Charles Kempe illustrating 'The Four Seasons'.

Folk say, a wizard to a northern king
At Christmas-tide such wondrous things did show,
That through one window men beheld the spring,
And through another saw the summer glow,
And through a third the fruited vines a-row,
While still, unheard, but in its wonted way,
Piped the drear wind of that December day.

4. The Sharington Range

After he acquired Dudley Castle from the debt-ridden John de Sutton, John Dudley set about an ambitious building programme. He commissioned Sir William Sharington to design impressive new private apartments which he named the Sharington Range after the architect. William Sharington had travelled in Italy and applied his knowledge of 16th century Italian Renaissance style to the new buildings. In 1750 a devasting fire broke out in the Sharington Range which was gutted. Dudley Castle became the familiar ruin it is today.

5. Bentley Hall

Bentley Hall was one of the places that hid Charles II after his defeat at the Battle of Worcester in 1651. He was sheltered by Royalist Colonel John Lane who owned the hall at the time. It was his sister, Jane Lane, who was to ensure that Charles escaped to Bristol disguised as her servant. Bentley Hall was demolished in 1929 after the area had been undermined for coal and the building was in danger of collapse. Its approximate location is commemorated by a cairn which was erected by Walsall Historical Association in 1934.

6. West Bromwich Manor House (Bromwich Hall)

Originally built by Richard de Marnham in the 13th century, the medieval timber-framed hall is the oldest part of the building. It was a moated manor house built around a courtyard. A chapel and gatehouse were added later. In the 19th century the buildings were converted to tenements and the original manor house was obscured by a more modern frontage. West Bromwich Corporation purchased the building in the 1950s and were responsible for restoring it. The Manor House is now part of Sandwell Museums.

7. John Wesley

The Oak House in Oak Road West Bromwich was the home of John Turton and his family in the mid-17th century. John was a yeoman (middle class) farmer who turned the Oak House into a gentleman's residence. In 1768 it was inherited by William Whyley. It was William who invited John Wesley, one of the founders of Methodism, to preach at Oak House. A plaque records that this took place on the 19th of March 1774 although this may not have been the only occasion he preached there.

8. Holbeche House

In 1605, the remaining gunpowder plotters made their way to Holbeche House after raiding Warwick Castle for fresh horses and obtaining a further supply of gunpowder from Hewell Grange in Redditch. The powder got damp and attempts to dry it in front of a damped down fire resulted in an explosion. This alerted the High Sheriff of Worcestershire who mounted a siege and killed or captured the remaining plotters apart from Robert Wintour and Stephen Lyttleton who went on the run.

9. The Lyttleton Family

The head of the Lyttleton family who live at Hagley Hall takes the title Viscount Cobham. The follies of Hagley Park were largely created by George Lyttleton in the 18th century. They include a 'mock' ruined castle designed by architect Saunderson Miller and a copy of a Greek Doric temple by James 'Athenian' Stewart. The

18th century obelisk on Wychbury Hill is visible for miles around and is a striking local landmark.

10. Pre-Raphaelite

William Morris was not directly involved with Wightwick Manor near Wolverhampton but his daughter, May Morris, was acquainted with Rosalie Glynn Grylls, the second wife of Sir George Mander. Together the couple created a remarkable collection of Pre-Raphaelite artwork, some of which was created by friends of William Morris. As well as work by artists such as Edward Burne-Jones and Ford Madox Brown there is work by women Pre-Raphaelite artists such as Lizzie Siddal.

People and places

Mythical beings, well-known people, buildings, and landmarks can all be found in this section. Memorials, particularly town clocks, are a familiar sight across the Black Country but less familiar these days are the people they were erected to commemorate.

1. Theophilus Dunn, who spent many years living in Netherton, was better known by what nickname?

2. Who was the former mayor and benefactor remembered all over West Bromwich including having the clock tower at Carters Green named after him?

3. The memorial clock in Willenhall is dedicated to the memory of which popular local doctor who died in 1891?

4. Although never used as such, Dudley Castle was surveyed as a possible residence to detain which high ranking prisoner?

5. With the industrial Black Country edging ever closer to Himley Hall, which stately home in Worcestershire was purchased by the Ward family in the 1830s?

6. The Georgian House situated above the Wolverhampton Wanderers Football Club ground was formerly a hotel and before that home to which prosperous family?

7. Wednesbury Clock Tower in the Market Place is a familiar sight but whose Coronation was it built to commemorate?

    a. Queen Victoria

    b. King Edward VII

    c. King George V

    d. King George VI

8. An old rhyme had Satan standing somewhere worse than Hell but where was it?

9. Joe Darby, the famous jumper, was once mistaken for which mythical character whilst practising jumps across the canal at night in Netherton?

10. Who was the Anglo-Saxon Princess of Mercia who is said to have constructed a defensive stronghold at Wednesbury?

Question 5 – Former home of the Ward family

Answers – Section 19

1. The Dudley Devil or Devil Dunn

Theophilus Dunn was known as a 'cunning man' and a prophet. He sold charms to cure toothache and other ailments, told fortunes and claimed to be able to find lost valuables. He was said to be an educated man as were many of his 'clients' who would come from far and wide to seek his advice. He is famously reputed to have predicted the outcome of William (Tipton Slasher) Perry's last fight which he lost against Tom Sayers:

> *Slasher, yo'll stop as yo' started.*
> *Yo'll get all yo' gi'ed in one goo;*
> *Yo' an' yer pub will be parted,*
> *Tom Little will mek it cum true.*

2. Reuben Farley

The 1897 Farley Clock Tower in Carters Green is a memorial to Alderman Reuben Farley. The inscription around the base reads, 'This tower was erected in recognition of the public services of Alderman Reuben Farley JP'. The Oak House in West Bromwich was purchased by Farley with the intention of making it his family home. Apparently, his wife took a dislike to it, and they never moved in. Farley then presented it to the town as a museum which opened in 1898 after careful restoration. Oak House Museum remains free to enter as Reuben Farley originally intended.

3. Dr Joseph Tonks

Born in Willenhall, Joseph Tonks qualified in medicine at Queen's College Birmingham in 1879. At a time when you had to pay to see a doctor, he was known as the 'poor man's doctor' for his efforts to ease the suffering of the poor in Willenhall. In 1888 he was involved in a ballooning accident at a local show. His injuries did not seem severe but nevertheless ultimately resulted in his death aged just 35 in 1891. A memorial clock tower and drinking fountain was erected by public subscription and unveiled in 1892.

4. Mary Queen of Scots

Catholic cousin to Queen Elizabeth I, Mary Queen of Scots fled to England in 1568 to seek refuge but instead was held in captivity. In the period 1585-6 she was in Staffordshire, firstly at Tutbury Castle, then Chartley Old Hall, and for a short time at Tixhall Hall. In 1585 Dudley Castle had been surveyed as a possible residence for the captive Mary, but was not deemed suitable. Queen Elizabeth herself had visited Dudley Castle ten years previously in 1575.

5. Witley Court

By the 1830s, the industrial Black Country was beginning to encroach on Himley Hall. The Trustees for the young William Ward (11th Baron Ward, created Earl of Dudley in 1860) purchased Witley Court, a stately home in Worcestershire. He did not move in immediately, but by 1860 had largely remodelled Witley into one of the grandest stately homes of England. Witley Court was sold in 1920 and sadly burnt down in 1937. The still magnificent ruins and fountains are now administered by English Heritage.

6. The Molineux Family

Before becoming a hotel in 1871, Molineux House was a fashionable residence. When it was built around 1820 it was on the outskirts of Wolverhampton with fine countryside views. Benjamin Molineux acquired the house in 1744 and it became the family home. The Molineux family had become wealthy through various business interests and could afford to have the house extended. It remained in the Molineux family until the mid-1850s when Wolverhampton had expanded, and the house was no longer in such a desirable location. The name remained when the building became a hotel and of course when the grounds became the Molineux Stadium, home to Wolverhampton Wanderers Football Club.

7. King George V

The clock tower in Wednesbury Market Place stands on the site of the former market cross building. It was built to commemorate the coronation of King George V in 1911. The clock tower was designed by a local architect, C. W. D. Joynson and paid for by the people of Wednesbury through a memorial fund. It is made of sandstone on red bricks and is Historic England Grade II listed.

8. Brierley Hill

This old rhyme illustrates very vividly the industrial landscape that had already grown up around the area at the time:

When Satan stood on Brierley Hill
And far around him gazed,
He said, "I never more shall feel
At Hell's fierce flames amazed."

The rhyme is thought to date back to the 18th century.

9. Spring Heeled Jack

In the mid-1800s, Spring Heeled Jack stories were rife across the country. This was a creature with glowing red eyes, cloven hooves and horns who would leap over buildings. In 1877 there were multiple witnesses to Spring Heeled Jack with just one bright shining eye jumping over the canal at Netherton in the dead of night. The local constabulary were called and bravely surrounded 'Jack'. They had actually apprehended champion jumper Joe Darby, who was practising his signature standing jump over the canal wearing a miner's helmet and lamp!

10. Ethelfleda (also known as Aethelflaed)

Wednesbury still remembers an Anglo-Saxon warrior princess known as the Lady of the Mercians in place names and artwork. Ethelfleda (also known as Aethelflaed) was the daughter of King Alfred the Great and sister to Edward the Elder. Legend has it that she fortified Wednesbury against the Danes. Together with her brother, Edward, she won a decisive battle against the Northern Danes at Wednesfield (also known as the Battle of Tettenhall) in the year 910.

Miscellany

This final section includes the questions that do not quite fit in anywhere else. From architecture to ironing with a bit of grave robbing thrown in for good measure, here are some more facets of this fascinating area known as the Black Country.

1. What was the Black Country name for body snatchers and grave robbers?

2. Dudley Zoo is home to a unique set of buildings designed by which group of Modernist architects led by Berthold Lubetkin?

3. In common with other hospitals in the Black Country, Walsall Manor started life in 1838 as what?

4. The industrial Black Country was never a particularly healthy place to live, but if you could afford it where might you have gone locally to 'take the medicinal waters' and supposedly improve your health and well-being?

5. Ironing used to involve heating sad irons on a trivet in front of the fire or on the kitchen range, but where did the name originate from?

6. Known locally as pepper pots, what purpose do these small brick structures serve?

7. What type of aerial craft made the Black Country's first powered flight in 1905?

8. The parish of Halesowen was severely affected by what between May and August of 1349?

9. Prior to 1857 what was the illegal alternative to divorce for poorer folk?

10. Dudley Borough Council experimented with cast iron houses in the 1920s only to find them too costly and so just four were ever built, but two of these can still be found where?

Question 2 – Dudley Zoo and Castle

Answers – Section 20

1. 'Diggum uppers'

By the late 18th century, medical schools were becoming more commonplace resulting in a serious shortage of corpses for dissection. This led to a brisk trade for the resurrectionists or 'diggum uppers' as they were known in the Black Country. They would dig up freshly buried corpses at night and then sell them on for medical dissection. It was not uncommon for family or friends of the deceased to mount a vigil over the grave to deter the 'diggum uppers'.

2. The Tecton Group

When Dudley Zoo was being created in the 1930s, Berthold Lubetkin and his Tecton Group of architects were commissioned to design buildings which fitted in with the hillside and also gave visitors unrestricted views of the animals. Thirteen such buildings were constructed of which twelve remain including the iconic undulating concrete entrance. All are listed buildings. There are animal enclosures, cafés, kiosks, and the Queen Mary Ballroom which was built to resemble an ocean liner.

3. A Workhouse

The 1834 Poor Law organised parishes into unions which were obliged to build workhouses for the needy poor. Although not prisons, life was harsh in the workhouses and poorer people would live in dread of having to go there. A new Walsall Union workhouse was built on Pleck Road in 1838. A large workhouse infirmary for sick inmates was opened in 1896. In the late 1920s control was passed from the Board of Guardians to Walsall Council who renamed the workhouse 'Beacon Lodge' and the workhouse infirmary 'The Manor Hospital'. The Board of

Guardians' offices for the old workhouse can still be seen preserved on Pleck Road in the grounds of Manor Hospital.

4. **Saltwells Spa**

Whilst not quite on a par with spa towns such as Bath, Cheltenham or even Droitwich, the Black Country had its own spa at Saltwells. It was located near Quarry Bank between Brierley Hill and Cradley Heath. Medicinal spring water supposedly flowed from the Lady Well, although renowned chemist and Lunar Society member James Keir was not impressed when he analysed it in 1798. Nevertheless, this didn't stop a bathhouse being erected over the spring in the early 1800s for the benefit of those taking the waters. The spa is no longer there but Saltwells is now a National Nature Reserve.

5. **Sad is Old English for solid**

Sad irons or flat irons were made of solid iron and came in various weights and sizes. They would be heated on the fire or range and ironing often took place on the kitchen table covered with a blanket and an old sheet on top. Correct temperature was important and the time-honoured way to check was to spit on the hot iron. If it sizzled and dried the temperature was just right. At least two irons would be needed so one was heating up whilst the other was being used.

6. **Canal tunnel ventilation**

Known locally as 'pepper pots' they are air vents which follow the line of the canal tunnel beneath. The nickname comes from their circular shape which generally resembles a table pepper pot. They are usually made of brick and topped by a domed metal grid, hence pepper pot. When passing through the tunnel below a shaft of light and usually drips of water denote the presence of a pepper pot above.

7. A powered airship

Stanley Spencer made one of the first ever engine powered sustained flights in the history of aviation over London on the 19th of September 1902 in a 75-foot airship called Mellin. In 1905, a demonstration of powered flight took place at a fête in the grounds of Corbett Hospital in Amblecote, Stourbridge. The successful ascent on the 7th of August 1905 was the first powered flight in the Black Country. The craft was a petrol engined, gas filled airship piloted by Stanley Spencer himself.

8. The Black Death

The Black Death, thought to have been Bubonic Plague, reached the Midlands area and the Black Country in the summer of 1349. Halesowen was particularly badly affected between May and August. Whilst other areas in the Black Country also suffered, Manorial Rolls kept by Halesowen Abbey for the period record a grim picture of the death toll there. In some cases, whole families were wiped out. Across the area which would later become the Black Country, estimates vary but between a third and half of the population perished in the plague.

9. Wife selling

In 1857 the Matrimonial Causes Act (Divorce Act) allowed divorce through a civil court instead of a Private Act of Parliament. In the Black Country as elsewhere wife selling, although illegal, was often considered socially acceptable amongst poorer folk. Very often, the wife, husband, and 'purchaser' were in agreement beforehand. A set ritual would be followed for the sale itself to satisfy all parties. After the sale it was customary to hold a celebration in any convenient public house. In one well documented case from Walsall Market in 1837, the wife had willingly set up home with the 'purchaser' long before the actual sale took place!

10. The Black Country Living Museum

An anticipated inter-war brick shortage in the 1920s led Dudley
Borough Council to experiment with cast iron houses. As houses
they were quick to build and comfortable, but the cost was
prohibitive, and the supply of bricks proved not to be a problem.
The cast iron houses were nearly twice the cost of conventional
brick. Only two pairs of semi-detached cast iron council houses
were ever built on the Brewery Fields Estate in Dudley. The
remaining pair are preserved at the Black Country Living
Museum.

About the Author

Andrew Homer has written several books on the Black Country and Birmingham and has an MA in West Midlands History awarded by the University of Birmingham. He is also a former Secretary of the Black Country Society. Andrew presents lectures to various organisations and has appeared on local and national television. After a career as a college lecturer, and prior to retirement in Devon, Andrew enjoyed working as a Historic Character at the Black Country Living Museum interpreting and explaining the history of the region and the stories of the people who helped to forge our industrial and social heritage.

Andrew can be contacted through his website at:

www.andrewhomer.co.uk

By the same author:

Secret Black Country - Amberley Publishing

A – Z of the Black Country - Amberley Publishing

A – Z of Birmingham - Amberley Publishing

Historic England: The Black Country - Amberley Publishing

Historic England: Birmingham - Amberley Publishing

Black Country Ghosts and Hauntings - Tin Typewriter Publishing

Beer and Spirits - Amberley Publishing

Haunted Hostelries of Shropshire - Amberley Publishing

A Black Country Miscellany - Tin Typewriter Publishing